SECRETS EVERY AUTHOR SHOULD KNOW

Indie Publishing Basics

MAGGIE MCVAY LYNCH

Windtree
Press

Frustrated with the plethora of conflicting information on how to self-publish? Wouldn't it be wonderful to sit down with someone who has already made the mistakes, done the analysis, and will provide you the short cuts—the secrets about the things that work? Now you have that chance with the *Career Author Secrets* series.

Indie Publishing (Self Publishing) has changed dramatically in the past five years. There are now new, easier tools to use for every part of the process—editing, formatting, distribution, sales, and analysis. This first book in the *Career Author Secrets* series provides a foundation for navigating the indie publishing process and staying away from the scammers. It breaks down the requirements for self-publishing successfully, protecting your rights for the future, and YES I do share all the secrets I've learned.

It contains everything a DIY author needs to get her book from manuscript to professional publication in both ebook and print, including:

- Why books don't sell
- Options for DIY or contracting professionals
- The truth about ISBNs & Copyright Registration
- Secrets for formatting your book the easy way
- Creating book covers that sell
- Making decisions about distribution

This book is especially valuable for those with limited technical skills who want to produce a quality professional book for the least amount of cost. BUY NOW and learn the secrets to easier implementation and how to make good decisions on what is worth your time and money.

Copyright © 2016 by **Maggie McVay Lynch**

All rights reserved. No part of this publication may be reproduced, distributed or transmitted in any form or by any means, without prior written permission.

Windtree Press

Hillsboro, Oregon

http://windtreepress.com

Cover Design by Christy Keerins

https://coveredbyclkeerins.com/

Contains several excerpts from

DIY Publishing by Maggie McVay Lynch

Copyright © 2013 by Maggie McVay Lynch

Secrets Every Author Should Know: Indie Publishing Basics / Maggie McVay Lynch. -- 1st ed.

Print ISBN 978-19449737-9-7

Ebook ISBN 978-19449730-8-7

United States of America

❦ Created with Vellum

*To all those authors who blazed the self-publishing trail
and eagerly shared their enthusiasm and learning
with the rest of us.*

Chapter One
INTRODUCTION TO INDIE PUBLISHING

"Write, write, and write some more." If content is king in developing a publishing strategy then a connected series is queen, and quality is the foundation for that empire. One repeated mantra is that Self Publishing is a marathon, not a sprint."
— Dianna Love, NYT and USA TODAY Bestselling Author

If you have come to this book with the idea that you can write a manuscript over a few months, share it with your closest friends, get someone with an English degree to check grammar, and then put it up on Amazon and sell millions, I'm afraid you will be sorely disappointed. Yes, you can put up anything you've written on Amazon, Kobo, Nook, Google Play, iBooks, and many more places with relative ease. You can announce it to the world on social media, and even go on blog tours to let everyone know how wonderful it is. But selling beyond your friends and family is NOT likely.

In the early days of self-publishing (2010-2012) there were a number of books that were poorly executed, but with good stories, that sold well. But those days are long gone. With over half a million indie books being put up every year, readers have become wary of trying new authors. They have formed mental checklists that help them determine if a new book is going to be worth their time. This list includes evaluating the cover, reading the blurb, checking the sample or "Look Inside" feature, checking the reviews, and looking at the author page to see what else he/she has written. To sell well today, you need to pass all those tests.

That is what this book is about—how to make your book the best it can be, how to package it so that people will at least click on the cover to learn more, and how to write descriptions that draw readers in and want to take a chance on an unknown author. Then once the reader takes a chance on you, you must deliver to their expectations—expectations for story, formatting, and navigation. AND, if the reader likes your book, they will want to immediately buy another book from you. If you don't have another book now, or coming soon, you will quickly be forgotten.

This first chapter will provide a quick overview of the entire publishing process to give you the scope of requirements. Subsequent chapters will then go into much more detail to ensure you can do this on your own and create/package the best book possible.

But before we get into that let's make sure we are on the same page in terms of understanding what indie publishing is all about and how it differs from traditional publishing.

Self-Publishing – This is a process by which an individual handles all the aspects of publishing his/her book. It does not necessarily mean she does it all herself. She may have a team of people she contracts. The key is she is the publisher.

Indie Publishing – This has become synonymous with "self-publishing." Over the past three years or so, this term is preferred by most people who self-publish. Anyone who takes on the tasks of publishing is an indie publisher.

This also applies to a person or group of people who form a publishing company outside of the major publishers and acquire books.

Independent publishing is nothing new. From Virginia and Leonard Woolf starting up Hogarth Press to the early days of Farrar, Straus and Giroux championing now-iconic authors that other publishers wouldn't touch, DIY publishing has long been responsible for some of our best literature. Today, you often see "indie presses" or "indie publishers" who represent poetry or certain niche markets not embraced by big publishers, like narrative history, memoirs, spiritual self-help, and niche markets for fiction.

Today, most small presses or niche presses call themselves "indie" publishers. This includes well-known literary publishers like Tin House, Melville House, and Coffee House Press to new presses that grew out of online zines, such as Ugly Duckling Press in Oregon now with over 200 titles. Also, genre presses such as Entangled, Aberdeen, Poisoned Pen, any many others.

What is the Process for Publishing?

Outside of the rise of digital books, the publishing process has been fairly well defined for 150 years. The chart below shows the publishing process for traditional books with the same thing for Indie books.

Process Step	Traditional Press (all done in-house)	Indie Press (self-publish)
Content submission	Author sends to editor or agent.	Author sends to beta readers or editor
Quality check	Acquiring editor determines if ms meets publishing house standards	Beta readers and/or developmental editor provides feedback on quality
Approval & Negotiation	Acquiring editor gets approval to make an offer and negotiates with author or agent	Author decides if she wants to put this book out, make changes, and what investment of time or money is appropriate
Editing	May include developmental editor, copy editor and proofreader	If developmental editor was used in quality check, author determines how to get copy edits and proofreading done
Book Design	Interior look & feel and cover design begins during editing process	Author designs interior and cover or contracts for one or both to be done
Sales & Marketing	Blurb, metadata, marketing copy created	Author determines or contracts out blurb, metadata, and marketing copy
Printing &	Print run is	Most indie authors

Let's Break Down These Steps to the Key Components

They key to indie publishing, just as in traditional publishing, is developing a team that you trust to do the jobs you can't or are not willing to do yourself. Although all the above items are handled in-house with traditional publishers and small presses, each person has a set of skills and things they know how to do. You need to develop that same approach.

For example, if you are a graphic designer in your day job and you know Adobe Photoshop inside and out, then you might feel comfortable taking on cover design yourself. Even if you are comfortable with the tools, you will still need to invest some time in learning how the design impacts your genre, your branding, if you are doing series etc. Designing book covers is a different knowledge base than designing a commercial brochure for a business.

If you have a good marketing background, you may be fine with developing a marketing plan and implementing it yourself. Again, you need to find out what works for selling books vs cars or houses or refrigerators.

For every aspect of the publishing process there are people available to help you implement it. The key is determining who they are, what you can afford, and whom you can trust. There are plenty of people out there who offer services not worth your time or money.

Content Submission – Judging Quality

One of the refrains I hear constantly from authors is: "If I get a contract from X publisher, I'll know the book is good enough to publish." The corollary to that for Indie authors is: "How do I know it's good enough?"

Let's back up a step. Before you send your manuscript to an editor or agent, how do you know it's good enough? You've probably shared it with your critique group. Perhaps you've some friends who read in your genre to read it and give you feedback. Perhaps you've entered it in some contests. All of these are viable to do for yourself as an indie publisher as well.

The step that an acquiring editor provides is a trained eye (one hopes) for what types of books, for that particular house, sells well. Note the words "for that particular house." This is why the same manuscript sent to multiple publishers will get different responses. That editor is not only judging your general prose writing and storytelling ability, she is also judging whether the book FITS their line.

You need to find someone similar for your Indie books. If you are writing a contemporary romance, then you need to find beta readers or a developmental editor who regularly reads and understands the contemporary romance genre. If you are writing a science fiction novel then you need to find someone who knows that genre. If you are writing a memoir... you get the picture. For beta readers you can cultivate a network of people through writer organizations, friends, or even making a request online. For editors, ask your friends who they use and then check out the costs and make sure that YOUR genre is listed in the types of books they edit.

Editing

No matter how good a writer you might be, you should NOT try to edit your own work. It doesn't matter if you teach English at a university or have a graduate degree in Creative Writing, you still should NOT rely only on yourself to edit your manuscript. Once you have written, edited, re-worked language, changed story, you are no longer an objective reader. When you read your completed manuscript it will say what you want it to say because you read your intention into your own words. Only an outside reader can tell you whether it is on the page and whether it makes sense.

There are three types of editors you need to concern yourself with. Yes, it is costly to use all three of them. However, for the best, finished manuscript you need these three edits in some form. Here are the three types.

Developmental Editor – This is someone who understands your genre, the expected tropes, the craft of story structure, character development, story and character arc, pacing, beats, description, foreshadowing, backstory—all the parts of a story that make a difference between a story your readers are likely to love vs a story that doesn't keep them engaged. Though some developmental editors will also make comments on line-edit or copy-edit things, this is not their primary function.

My developmental editor will call out voice, word choice, and sentence construction problems when she notices it. But we have an understanding that she won't notice all of them and I should not rely on her for copy edits. If my story needs a lot of work, she won't notice the line edit stuff. Where my story is working well on it's own she is more likely to see line edit needs.

Copy Editor or Line Editor – This person is the line-by-line checker. She concentrates primarily on consistency of voice, punctuation, grammar, character and plot. A copy editor may suggest different phrasing, some word choices, and sentence structure based on YOUR voice and approach to the story. For example, if your character tends to speak in short sentences with pauses represented by ellipses and always uses modern vernacular, the copy editor will call out the dialog that goes on and on and sounds more formal or descriptive as being inconsistent with your voice or the character's voice. In addition, the copy editor might include fact-checking, spelling, consistent formatting on a chapter-by-chapter basis and, if there is a "house style," make sure that your manuscript meets that style.

Proofreader - A proofreader is the one who goes over your manuscript after an editor. She looks for things that were missed during the editing process. This tends to include punctuation, spelling, and formatting. The proofreader should not be making word choice changes, plot changes, character changes etc. She is simply making sure the manuscript is clean.

So, who do you need to hire? If you want your manuscript to be as perfect as possible, you really need to hire all three of these folks. However, if you are just starting out you may find you are only able to afford one editor. If that is the case then hire the developmental editor. The STORY is important above all else. If the story is in great shape, a reader will forgive the occasional grammar or punctuation error. However, if you have a perfect clean manuscript but the story doesn't hold up, it will not be forgiven.

There are a number of other ways you can get sufficient (though not great) line edits and proofreading with a combination of beta readers, exchanges, and even software. But most beta readers and other authors will not be good developmental editors.

Book Design

Book Design includes two parts—the book interior and the cover. Some decisions about the interior are:

How will fonts define the look and feel – header, subheader, body, setting, special sections (i.e., old scroll text, a different language, mindspeak)

How will you show scene change, POV change? This is often done either with blank space, small caps, or dividers. Dividers can be as simple as asterisks or a hash mark. Or the divider can be some type of image or special character. For example, in a children's book about a shelter dog the divider was a paw print. In a thriller about an assassin, the divider was a gun scope target.

What will be included in the front matter? The back matter? Will the font for that be different than the primary narrative font?

If the book contains images or illustrations, what size will they be? Will they be placed on a facing page or integrated with the text?

Some decisions for the cover design include:

- What is acceptable for the genre in terms of images, colors, over all look and feel? For example, contemporary romances tend to have lighter color washes, whereas thrillers are darker. Some genres are character focused and have people as the central image. Other genres have no people on the cover.
- Is this part of a series? If so, what needs to be the same on every book in the series to signal that? Some series carry the title or tagline in a specific place on every book. Some series uses the same color scheme while others use a different color for each book but the same types of images.
- How does it work with the author brand? For example, is the author's name always in a Trajan font and at the bottom? Is the author brand light or dark? Sweet or sexy? Literary or genre?
- How does the book look the same, or different, from the author's other books? If the author writes in more than one genre, how does she differentiate that to the reader and yet stay true to her brand?
- Is there a publisher branding? If you have a publishing company name, is there a logo that needs to appear on the front cover? The spine? The back cover?
- If a print book, how are the primary images and colors going to meld into the spine and back cover? How is the spine designed? Title on top, author name on bottom or reverse? Is there a publisher logo? How long is the blurb and is it consistent from one book to another? Will you indicate the price as part of the ISBN?

Sales & Marketing

Sales & Marketing actually has several components as well. 1) Preparing and implementing the metadata; 2) Defining a review plan; 3) Determining distribution; 4) Sending out ARCs; 5) Choosing a launch plan—soft or hard or both? 6) Creating a marketing budget; 7) Implementing both free and paid marketing plans on a schedule; 8) Follow up on all sales and marketing efforts to determine next steps.

Preparing and Implementing Metadata - This part of publishing is much more than sending out ARCs and advertising. The metadata is the information about the book that will help indexers and search engines to "discover" the book when a reader is looking. Without good metadata, no one will find your book no matter how well it is written.

Metadata includes the title, subtitle, book description, keywords, category selection, reviews, author bio, author name, and any thing else associated with the book. For example how you write that book description can make a big difference in sales. It is not as much about describing the story by plot or character as it is about hooking the reader within the first two sentences. Choosing categories are critical to discoverability. Defining the category to be small enough that YOUR readers can discover you, yet large enough that it is still found by people who like the genre in general. Finally, selecting keywords that readers will actually use. You may thing that the year 1920 is important to the book, but will a reader ever type that in? Or would she instead type in "roaring 20's?"

Defining a Review Plan – What types of reviews do you want and in what timeframe? Will you be pursuing critical or editorial reviews from magazines, newspapers, and specific reviewers with a lot of cache (i.e., Publishers Weekly, Kirkus, a major magazine like the New Yorker) What about book bloggers or genre magazines? If you are going for actual reader reviews, how will you find those readers and how will you follow up with them once they have left a review? For readers, where do you want the review to appear? (Amazon, Apple, Kobo, Nook, Goodreads, Twitter, FB, Pinterest, etc.) Is there a time frame in which the review must be done if they receive a free copy?

How will you use the reviews to drive more traffic to your book? Will you add them to your website? Will you talk about them on social media? Will you simply let them talk for themselves and hope readers fine them?

Determining Distribution – Are you doing both ebook and print? If so, where will you be loading/sending your finished book and in what timeframe? Will you go exclusive to one vendor, like Amazon? Or will you distribute widely to multiple vendors? Are you going to load to each distributor yourself, or will you use an aggregator (e.g., Draft 2 Digital, Smashwords, Book Baby, Vearsa) to distribute for you? How will you make sure the book is in the proper format for loading for each distributor? What are the delays from loading a book to it's actual appearance in a catalog or on a vendor website? How will your launch plan match with those delays? What kinds of metadata does each vendor require/allow and how you will match that at the time books are loaded?

Sending Out ARCs – ARCs are advanced reader copies. This can be print copies of your book, or ebook copies. Certain genres require print copies from most reviewers (e.g., non-fiction with tables or illustrations), whereas other genres accept ebooks (e.g., romance and SF). You need to have a list of people who have agreed to receive the ARCs and in exchange will do something that will help push the book. This might be reviews, mentions, simply posting book information, or all of the above.

ARCs can be sent to fans in exchange for an honest review, to specific reviewers/bloggers, and to anywhere or anyone who influences readers' purchases like newspapers and booksellers. You also need a way to follow up with those people to determine if a review is done, where it's posted or when it will appear and how that impacts the rest of your marketing plan.

Choosing a Launch Plan – There are numerous ways to launch a book. The easiest and least costly is what is called a "soft" launch. That means the book gains momentum incrementally. It begins by uploading the book everywhere. Adding it to your website. Perhaps doing an FB post or Tweet about it being available, and putting it in your newsletter. You don't do a lot of "selling" or marketing. You don't by ads.

A "hard" launch is a planned launch with specific dates that things will happen—all designed to gain velocity over a short period of time. For example, you might begin talking about the book everywhere a month before it comes out. Two weeks before you would be emailing your readers, tweeting, FB posts. You would schedule a book signing or party the day of the launch and plan follow up marketing for each day. A hard launch requires a lot more planning, and money in order to get the news out to as many as people as possible. Because today's digital world is based on algorithms, the sustained effort over a week or a month can make a big difference in sales.

The "combination launch" is my choice. Begin with a soft launch. That means go ahead and mention it to your friends, family, mailing list fans and do a couple of tweets. This is giving the book time to build reviews and giving the vendor algorithms time to kick in as a few sales here and there occur. A decent number of sales and reviews will make you look more impressive when you get to the hard launch maybe a month or two later.

Also, if this is your first book, it gives you time to get any feedback regarding spelling, grammar, and formatting. This is particularly important if you were not able to invest in editing and proofreading. Better to get that information and make changes before a thousand people know about the book.

A soft launch gives you time to get the book on all your Internet sites—website, blog, social media, adding it to your Amazon Author Central page and Goodreads author page. Sometimes in the run up to release, these things are missed or quickly forgotten if you are running a hard launch that is taking all of your energy.

Once the book has been out for a month or more, started to gain reviews and purchases, then you will have a basis by which to do a hard launch. Then when people go to all the possible sites to learn about your new book it will be ready and you will be ready and able to devote the time needed to juggle all the balls.

Distribution and Launch

Now that you've done all the hard work of preparation, you are ready to launch. That means you now physically load the book to all the vendors you've selected, include the appropriate metadata and implement your chosen launch plan. Remember, your book will not show up at every vendor at the same time. For example, loading to Amazon the book will show up within 24 hours—usually more like two hours. Loads to Nook or Kobo can be anywhere from 24 hours to 72 hours. Apple iTunes is usually 48 hours.

If you are loading a print book to Createspace, the print book will show on all Amazon sites within 24-48 hours. However, it will not appear on the expanded sites (B&N, Book Depository, Books A Million, Indiebound, etc.) for up to six weeks later. This is critical to understand for your marketing efforts as well.

If you are using Ingram Spark, it can be up to two weeks from the time you load the book until it appears in the Ingram Catalog and again up to six weeks before it shows up on other book sites (same one as above).

Yikes! I'm Overwhelmed

All of this may feel overwhelming. This is why I began with describing the team concept. If you try to do it all yourself it IS overwhelming and it will severely impact your ability to write the next book. This is particularly true if you have a lot of learning to do around these topics and need to schedule courses or self-teaching time.

Most indie authors choose to do certain parts themselves, such as the marketing and launch, while hiring or bartering for the other services they need. For example, I pay for a developmental editor and a cover designer. I know that those two areas are critical to the quality of my books and to being discovered. So, I budget to pay for those experts. I do not pay for marketing, distribution, or launches. I handle that myself. I took time (and continue to take time) to learn through classes and to understand what more I can do and how to get it done.

I personally believe that even though I may have someone else do some of the work, I still need to have a full understanding of what works and what doesn't so that I can supervise that person. For example, I currently have a part time virtual assistant who handles some of my social media and basic marketing/contest fulfillment efforts. I found that doing it myself took far too much time away from writing. However, I tell her what to do, make decisions and branding and marketing campaigns, focus of social media posts, etc. I couldn't do this if I didn't already understand what needs to be done, what works and what doesn't work for my readers and me.

The step-by-step DIY Publishing Process Summary

1. Select (or design) a template for print.
2. Apply that template to your finished manuscript.
3. Including appropriate front matter and back matter.
4. Add links for other ebook/print book titles you might have and make decisions around placement of front matter and additional back matter.
5. Import the finished manuscript into a conversion software package to generate appropriate ebook-compatible files and/or print book files, or paying someone, or using an aggregator or vendor/distributor to do the conversion for you.
6. Incorporate good cover design elements for print and ebook and create front a cover, spine, and back cover.
7. Write the book blurb and author bio, and use them effectively in marketing.
8. Set up distribution accounts in the major distributor sites (e.g., Amazon, CreateSpace, B&N, Kobo, Apple, etc.), and/or evaluate aggregators to use to distribute everywhere for you (Draft2Digital, Smashwords, StreetLib, Book Baby, XinXii).
9. Determine how and where to use ISBNs—the pros and cons of purchasing your own versus accepting each distributors inventory record assignments or proprietary ISBNs.
10. Upload your finished ebook and print files to each distributor or aggregator.

11. Set list prices and determine when and how to use sales to increase discoverability.
12. Make changes to books once they are with distributors. When should you just leave it alone?
13. Increase book discoverability, managing sales expectations, and becoming part of the zeitgeist of publishing today.
14. Create and implement a marketing/branding program and a book maintenance/update policy to ensure your books continue to attract readers.

This book is going to cover all of the above, except details on marketing and distribution. Those fields have grown exponentially since I wrote the DIY Publishing book in 2012-2013. So, they each have a book of their own devoted to all the options for authors today.

Now that you have the overview, let's look at things in more detail. The next chapter shares the top craft reasons books don't sell and provides some resources for you to make your book better.

CHAPTER TWO
CRAFT DOES MATTER

Craft Does MatterTop 5 Reasons
Books Get Bad Reviews
or Not Even a Look

#1 **Book blurb is boring, too long or doesn't meet genre expectations**

In today's technological world, readers make a decision very quickly about whether to try a new author or a new genre. Internet research tells us that the average purchaser spends all of 3-6 seconds on a product page before making a decision whether to click on a larger description or take a chance. Assuming at least two of those second is deciding if the cover is intriguing, that leaves only four seconds to read your blurb. If you don't catch the reader at the very beginning, they won't take the other ten second to finish reading and then make a decision.

You've probably seen the blurbs that follow all the "rule of four parts." Describe the situation. Describe the problem. Provide hope. Summarize the mood/theme. Um...I don't agree. All of this is tell, tell,

tell and you see millions of blurbs that follow this direction. And too many are long—three or four long paragraphs. Today's online shopper will never get through that. You need to stand out. Grab the reader by the throat and say, "Look at me. You'll rue the day you passed me by."

Your book's first line needs to say, "I'm intriguing. I'll give you more than you can imagine. Do you dare to try me?"

How do you do that? Some people do it with what is known as a "logline" or "tagline." That's a single sentence that encapsulates your story. Here are some of my loglines.

"Forgiving yourself is the first step, but helping others forgive may be just too hard." – This is a character problem line that summarizes the entire arc of the protagonist. This tells the reader this is a character-driven book.

"Children with no birth records and a soldier with PTSD together must define the value of human life." – This is a plot logline. It summarizes the entire plot and the thematic question. It tells the reader that this is going to be plot driven but also have characters that will strive to answer the thematic question.

You don't always have to use a logline as your first sentence. But trying to come up with one is a great exercise. If not a logline then start with the most intriguing part of your story. It may be the character. It may be the setting. It may be something that immediately tells the reader the genre.

Here is an example from my first book in a YA Fantasy series.

"Camryn Painter is a 16-year-old freak of nature. Or possibly the savior of a

civilization that isn't supposed to exist. She's a human chameleon... one who transforms into the image of whoever she sees."

In these three short sentences an intriguing character is established. The over-arching problem she faces is established. And the reader immediately knows it is in the fantasy or paranormal genre.

There are many more parts of writing a blurb. I would challenge you to try getting the most important part of your blurbs down to 100 words total. And make the first 50 the most important. Make every line count. Make it so that the reader must pick up that book.

Not all people are good at this. It is really hard to take a 200 or 300 page book and summarize it in 100 words that will make the reader say: "Wow! This sounds interesting." Fortunately, there are people who are very skilled at this and can write them for you. A number of marketing folks will write these. To my knowledge, there is only one person I know who focuses on writing blurbs, taglines, and calls to action for authors. She is quite popular and prices are reasonable. The Blurb Queen, Cathryn Cade

Some editors also provide a service for writing blurbs. One I know and recommend is The Literary Midwife, Mary Rosenblum

#2 Nothing Happens in the First 20-30 pages

You know that "Look Inside" feature that several distributors use? Or the "sample pages" in the case of Apple? If a reader gets past your blurb, the next thing she'll do is click on that sample. That sample is 20% or less of your book. That means with every page turn the reader is evaluating if it's interesting enough to continue. If you use those first pages to set up the book, tell the backstory, give a walking tour of the location, it is highly likely the reader won't even get through the entire sample.

You've probably heard, "start with action." That doesn't mean start with a bomb blast or someone dying (though you can). What it means is start with the point at which everything changes for your protagonist. There's a phrase called "walking to the story" that some editors use. It means you are doing a lot of writing before you actually get to where the story starts.

Even though all that information is important to your process, or to trying to let the reader know how your protagonist found herself in this mess, it is not doing you any favors in getting someone to pick up your book.

<u>All Writer Workshops</u> has several courses on craft to help you with this. Their workshops include character development, plot development, pacing, story structure, and special workshops on writing blurbs and taglines.

There are also a number of good writing craft books to help with your story development. My favorites are:

Break Into Fiction by Mary Buckham and Dianna Love
Practical Emotional Structure by Jodi Henley
Techniques of the Selling Writer by Dwight Swain
Self-Editing for Fiction Writers by Rennie Brown.

I admit the last one is the one I go back to at the end of every first draft fiction manuscript I write. I use it as a checklist for both developmental editing and good writing techniques. After I do that next edit (and sometimes a third edit), then I finally send my manuscript to a professional editor.

#3 No Story

I know that every writer believes she has written a great story—one that does everything she wanted it to do. And it is probably true. The problem comes when someone, other than the author, reads the story and doesn't see the same thing the author sees. This happens more often than I can count.

I've read entire 300+ page manuscripts that on a sentence-by-sentence level were beautifully written, had no typos or grammar problems, described and set up scenes and had decent dialog. But, after slogging through 300 pages, nothing really happened. The plot may have moved from point A to point B, but there was never real conflict or no one was really in jeopardy. The hero and heroine may have ended up in-love or married, but I never saw the relationship build and it all came too easily. The detective figured out the mystery by page 329, but it was already obvious to me by page thirty.

This is why no author should ever edit her own work as a final edit. By the time I finish a book, I am the last person who knows whether I really got everything across. In my mind I did. In my mind the stakes were high, the conflict was real, and the emotions were undeniable.

After more than 30 short stories, 15 novels, and 5 non-fiction books you'd think I have this down and wouldn't need an editor. Um…No… Not really. Yes, most of the book is okay. Yes, every manuscript is better because I carry what I learned before to this one.

However, EVERY time I send it to my Developmental Editor she finds more than one place where things are not so obvious to her as a reader. EVERY time I send a book out to Beta readers, there are several places where things are not so amazing as it is in my mind.

You may have a great cover and a book blurb (description) that draws readers to try you. However, books that fail to find a larger audience often have story craft problems. Even if readers don't tell YOU about it, they do share it among themselves or they list your book as DNF (did not finish) on places like Goodreads.

Some of those story craft problems are addressed in the classes and book resources I mentioned in item #2. A good Developmental Editor can address all of them. A developmental editor can identify problems with things like story and character arcs, themes, emotion, plot, pacing, scene and sequel, dialog, genre cookies, and many others. Do remember that not all editors are created equal. Also that, particularly in fiction, it is critical that your editor knows your genre inside and out. Reader expectations for romance books are very different from reader expectations for mysteries and those are different than science fiction.

In my opinion, if you have to choose only one editor, a good Developmental Editor is your best choice.

If you cannot afford a developmental editor then try to barter with someone. At least be sure to send your book to critique partners AND Beta Readers. Beta readers are people who read regularly in your genre. They are people you do not know personally and therefore will give you their honest answers.

Not sure who to hire as a developmental editor? Here are some I can recommend. Be sure to check out their websites and what types of books they are comfortable reading/editing. Most good developmental editors have specific genres they know well. It takes a great deal of constant research and reading to stay up on the requirements for all genres.

Some editors are writers themselves, and have a track record of success. However, there are also good editors who are only editors. Not all editors have a secret desire to be a writer. Ask around. Get recommendations from authors you admire. Ask any potential new editor to do a 10-page sample edit, so you can get a feeling for what types of things he/she will find and recommend. This person needs to get your voice and direction, and you will be spending a lot of time with your editor. So, select carefully.

[The Literary Midwife](), Mary Rosenblum
[Red Circle Ink](), Jessa Slade
[Jodi Henley](), Developmental Editor

There are also two advanced writing books I would highly recommend
Stein on Writing by Sol Stein – the most comprehensive book on actual techniques from plot to character to pacing and everything else that I've ever read.

Story Engineering by Larry Brooks – this goes beyond the basics of plot and structure into the parts that make it hang together or not

#4 Typos and Obvious Grammar Problems

If you succeed in getting to that purchase stage, and your story is well developed with characters a reader loves, the reader will forgive the occasional typo or grammar problem. But they will not forgive a lot of them.

If you deliver a book riddled with typos and grammatical errors you will be called out on it. Believe me, there are many readers who go looking for that and immediately post a review about it. Some will hold the book up for ridicule.

There are several ways to deal with proofreading. One way is to pay or barter with a professional proofreader. This is different from a developmental editor or a copy editor. A proofreader is someone who looks at every word, every punctuation mark, and every verb-tense agreement and finds the problems. She doesn't look at character arcs or plot development or make comments on whether there is enough emotion on the page. Like developmental editors, proofreaders have a specific skill set and great attention to detail. Most developmental editors admit they are NOT good proofreaders. So you do need to find someone else to do this.

I do understand that many writers on a budget have to choose only one editor. If that is the case, definitely choose the Developmental Editor. Then I would suggest a couple of options for proofing. 1) Find a friend who loves you and is the one who always catches typos in other books; 2) Use a service like [Autocrit](#) or [Pro Writing Aid](#). Software isn't perfect, but it's darn good and never gets tired reading your manuscript five or six times. This isn't as good as a human, but it does a decent job, and it is definitely better than doing nothing at all or relying on yourself to proofread. The key to using these tools is understanding how to fix the things it finds or when to ignore the advice.

#5 Reader Cookies

All readers come to a book with a set of expectations, and if those expectations are not met they are disappointed and either leave middling to bad reviews or simply don't come back for other books. Fulfilling these expectations are what I call "reader cookies." Those expectations are formed by three things: 1) Your promise in the blurb;

2) The categories/genres you select when you load the book; and 3) Tropes of the genre.

Your promise in the blurb. When you read the loglines I presented for three different books, it is likely that you formed an idea in your mind around what that book might contain. These ideas are based on your previous reading experiences with similar themes or ideas.

Though you cannot please every person who picks up your book, you also have to be very aware of what expectations you are setting up with your blurb. And then you MUST deliver on those expectations in the story. If you are setting up an emotional, character-driven story in your blurb then you better deliver that story. This means you have to have a strong sense of your protagonist and that character drives everything, from plot to black moment to resolution. If you are setting up a world, as I did in my fantasy blurb, then you better deliver something that is an entire world with a set of rules and societies, economics and power distribution, that is consistent throughout your book or series.

The Categories/Genres You Select. When you load your book to distributors you have to choose the categories that best fit your book. This is often hard for writers because many writers have a hard time deciding where it really fits.

Readers search based on those genre categories. If a reader is looking for a romance and your book is categorized that way, then you better deliver some romance tropes and have a happily-ever-after (HEA) at the end. If you fail to have the romantic relationship at the center of the story or you don't deliver an HEA, your reviews will reflect that problem and it will get around this really isn't a romance.

Every genre has "rules" about what belongs in that genre. Even non-fiction has these breakdowns. Expectations in a self-help book are different than expectations in a memoir.

If your book isn't selling, and you've done everything else right, knowing and selecting the right categories can make the difference. Book 3 in the Career Author Secrets series, **_Secrets to Pricing and Distribution_**, goes into category selection in detail and the metadata of keywords.

Once you have your story down, have it edited and proofread, you will next move to the packaging stage. Packaging your book is more than formatting your manuscript and putting it up. You need to determine what you want in front matter (before the story begins). What you want to put in back matter (after the story ends). These decisions can be critical to your marketing efforts, building your mailing list, and getting readers to come back for your next book.

Chapter Three
FRONT MATTER

Every book contains content prior to when the narrative starts (front matter) and after it ends (back matter). The placement of this content will vary depending on the format of the book. Print books have a traditional way of presenting information, beginning with the title page, copyright page, the dedication, and then the beginning of the primary content. Ebooks do not need to follow that same tradition. In fact, many ebook authors believe that most of the front matter should be placed at the back of the book in order to present the best information to draw readers in through sample pages or the "look inside" feature on many online purchasing sites.

It is the author's decision. Let's look at what is included and why, as well as the pros and cons for placement. Front matter refers to any content that comes prior to the main story or narrative. The traditional types of front matter include:
- Title Page
- Copyright Page
- Author Letter
- Foreword
- Table of Contents

- Dedication
- Acknowledgments

Many authors choose to only include the Title Page, Copyright page and Dedication from the list above. They then add the following in front matter.

- ***The back cover blurb or book description*** follows the title page. This is important because readers forget what the book was about if they don't read it right away. By repeating the book description, the reader is immediately reminded why they chose the book, the genre, and what to expect.
- ***Advance praise and pull quotes***. This is what is called "social proof." Having review excerpts or pull quotes from famous authors in your genre informs the reader that someone besides the author, her marketer, or immediate family has good things to say about the book.
- **A listing of other books by the author**. You want your reader to know that you are not a one-book author. Some publishers use the list in the front matter as social proof, while others prefer the list to be in back matter as a way to draw the reader to purchase more books. Some authors choose to put the list in both places.

Because of the page samples and look-inside features in online sales site, it is important to put the information in that will most draw your reader into purchasing the book. We will talk more about this in the ***Secrets to Effective Author Marketing*** book. Each of these elements serves a specific purpose. From the list above, the only required pages are the title page and the copyright page. I will discuss each page, its traditional purpose, and what options you might consider in electing to include that page or not and where to place it in your book.

The Title Page

The title page is important to reinforce the book title, author name, and publisher. If it is a print book and the cover has been torn or is missing, the title page still contains the information. If it is an ebook, depending on how the ebook files were constructed or the type of device used to read the electronic file, it is possible that the cover is not a part of the transmitted file. Thus the title page again serves as a means to identify the book.

In print books, the book's title is typically presented on the title page using the same font presented on the cover. If a subtitle is included, it would be centered below the main title. If the book is part of a series, the series title will then follow as the third item. A number of spaces then separate the titling section from the author's name, which usually appears near the center of the vertical page. Finally, centered toward the bottom are the publisher's name, city, state, and country.

This is not always the case. Take the time to peruse six or seven books by different publishers in order to review the choices they make. You will see that some only include the title on the title page, while others may include the publisher's name but not the location information.

In ebooks the above is also true for the title page, except the font used on the cover is often not available to be used in an ebook or will not display in the same manner. When I create an ebook, I attempt to keep the font as close to the cover as possible simply to make it stand out. However, I do understand that some ereaders will translate the font to Times Roman and there is nothing I can do about it. Another option is to make an image of the title page from your print book, with the fonts and styling you want, and use that as your title page in your ebook.

Copyright Page

The primary purpose of this page is to describe who owns the rights to the book and what, if anything, a person who buys a copy of the book can do with it. The copyright page also serves as the place where the publisher (you) provides bibliographic and contact information. Select three or four books from your library and examine the copyright pages. As I describe the elements identify where those are in your sample print or ebooks.

Though most copyright pages take up an entire page, the requirements are minimal. According to the United States Copyright office, you must include only three items:
- The symbol ©; the word "copyright"; or the abbreviation "Copr."
- The year of first publication. If the work is derivative or a compilation that incorporates previously published material, the year of first publication of the derivative work or compilation is sufficient.
- The name of the copyright owner.

For detailed information on the requirements review http://www.copyright.gov/circs/circ03.pdf .

The copyright information must appear in one of the following places:
- The title page
- The page immediately following the title page
- Either side of the front or back cover
- The first or the last page of the main body of the work

The most important element is the actual copyright statement which consists of three elements: the word Copyright or the symbol ©; the year of the first publication of the work; and identification of the copyright owner (you or your company) by name. Typically, these three elements together look like this.

Copyright 2016 by Maggie McVay Lynch
or
© 2016 by Maggie McVay Lynch
or
Copyright © 2016 by Maggie McVay Lynch

The final example is the one used by most print book publishers. In the case of an ebook, the copyright symbol may not always display correctly. In that case, using the first example without the symbol is sufficient.

Although there is no "legal" requirement to display a copyright statement, it is highly recommended. It serves a reminder that you recognize you are the owner of the copyright and states clearly that things cannot be copied or used without your permission.

In addition to the three elements of a copyright declaration mentioned above, there are other things you will want to include to meet the purposes of clarifying rights and providing contact and bibliographic information. It is also wise to include the book title, the ISBN, location of publication, reservation of rights statement, and contact information. The contact information may be as simple as a website address, or as complex as a complete mailing address.

Your new copyright page with this additional information might look like this example.

Copyright © 2016 by Maggie McVay Lynch
    Secrets Every Author Should Know: Indie Publishing Basics

ISBN 978-19449730-8-7
    United States of America

All rights reserved.
    For permissions contact: maggie@maggielynch.com

Given that the above is all that is required and suggested, why would an author want to include anything else? Let's review the additional elements most often found on publisher copyright pages. Some of these may apply to you and others may not. However, it is important to understand what each element is and why you might choose to include it.

Book Edition. If this is the first time the book has appeared in any format, it is the first edition. If the edition is not listed, it is assumed this is the first edition. However, some publishers like to make this explicit. Also, some publishers like to differentiate the format. For example: "First print edition" or "First ebook edition".

Note: If the book was published previously by another publisher, and you had the rights returned to you, you are now publishing a second edition with a new ISBN. The fact this is a second edition should be included on the copyright page. If you made substantial changes to the book and are now redistributing it (e.g., you added several new chapters or did a major rewrite), the book may be considered a new edition.

Expanded Rights Statement. Most publishers include an expanded rights statement that is a paragraph of information instead of the simple "All rights reserved" statement. Though this is not required, they want to be sure anyone reading the statement is clear on exactly what "all rights reserved" means. In addition, some ebook aggregators or distributors, like Smashwords, may require you to include them in your copyright page in order to be distributed by them.

Here is a typical example of an expanded all rights reserved statement.

All rights reserved. No part of this publication may be reproduced, distributed or transmitted in any form or by any means, including photocopying, recording, or other electronic or mechanical methods, without the prior written permission of the publisher, except in the case of brief quotations embodied in critical reviews and certain other noncommercial uses permitted by copyright law.

Acknowledgment or Credit to Contributors. This is where you would list your cover designer, editor, interior book designer, or others who were part of creating this book. Though these listings are not required, I believe it is good form and richly deserved to credit those individuals who help to make a difference in getting your book formatted and ready for publication.

Note: This is different from the people you acknowledgment who supported your efforts both emotionally and factually (e.g., critique partners, friends, family, etc.). Those individuals are credited in your acknowledgments or dedication.

In the copyright page for this book I acknowledged the cover designer for the book because the cover design is a separately copyrighted entity. Though I paid the designer for my cover, and I paid for the photo images used, the way in which the design is executed, placed on the page, font selections, etc. all belong to her.

Permission Statements. If you were required to get permissions to include certain types of details in your book, this is where those permissions are stated. For example, if I am writing a technology book and use screenshots of software I will get permission from the developer to use the screenshots. I would then acknowledge that permission on the copyright page. For a work of fiction, you may have sought and received written permission to use words from a song or specifics about a local restaurant. If you received written permission, this would be the place to acknowledge those things.

Publisher's Address and Contact Information. Larger publishers always want their information on the copyright page. This is a part of branding books and making a statement on quality related to the publisher. It also provides a way for anyone needing rights permissions to contact the publisher.

As discussed later in this book, I am an advocate of authors

forming a publishing company as the legal entity for holding all their publications. This can be as simple as a DBA, or as complex as creating a corporation. Whether you do that as an individual or as part of a group of authors, it provides a means to separate you as an individual from the public information on location and business correspondence. If you decide to create a publishing entity, you will want to provide that information just below the rights statement.

If you don't wish to form a separate publishing entity or join one, then the previous example of providing an email address or your own physical address is sufficient. It is definitely recommended that you provide some means by which you can be contacted for permissions. After all, you want to make it easy for those seeking translation rights, movie rights, or game rights to find you and negotiate.

Ordering Information. This only applies if you are engaging in direct sales through your website or a publishing website. Publishers will provide order information for large quantities or special discounts. Though this applies primarily to print books, it is possible you would also want to make discounts available for multiple orders of ebooks as well. For example, perhaps you wish to allow school classrooms to order your young adult ebook for use on school iPads at a discount. The language for ordering information is typically similar to that below.

Ordering Information:
    Quantity sales. Special discounts are available on quantity purchases by corporations, associations, booksellers, and others. For details, contact the "Special Sales Department" at the address above.

The "address above" language refers to the contact information described as the publisher's address.

Cataloging-in-Publication Data (CIP). This is data received from the Library of Congress for participating publishers. (Note: This may differ significantly in countries outside the U.S. depending on how they catalog data for their libraries) Most self-publishers cannot participate in this program. However, author publishing cooperatives may want to consider this. There is no fee to get the data. The requirements are for a publisher to have a minimum of three titles by three different authors in addition to the one being requested for cataloging. Publishers send information to the Library of Congress in advance of publication in order to get the cataloging data. Once the book is published, the publisher must send one copy to the Library of Congress. It is the receipt of this copy that replaces any fees.

NOTE: You are NOT required to have CIP data or MARC data in order to be in a library. What this does do is make it easier for a library to choose your book because the work will not have to be done by a librarian to get you in the catalog and electronic database.

Most self-publishers are precluded from using this service. However, the Library of Congress does have another option called PCIP or Publisher CIP that is used to get cataloging PRIOR to publication. This cataloging service is offered by other commercial entities that submit on your behalf. It requires an ISBN. The cost typically runs around $60-$80 per book. The downside is that the Library of Congress does not include these books in their weekly updates to libraries. However, other library entities (e.g., WorldCat) do and, depending on the private cataloger they may have authorization to upload your information to these other entities.

Is it worth it? It all depends on the library, the staffing, and their policies on stocking books that have been donated or purchasing books. You can wait and see if a library purchases your book and creates the catalog entry for it. Once a library creates an entry it is shared with other libraries to use. Then you can use that in the future. Even if you donate a book to a library, or get them to purchase it, it may still take months before the book is actually shelved because of the cataloging requirement. Cataloging often goes to the bottom of a busy librarian's to-do list. Having this information in your book makes it easier for them and more likely to get it on the shelves quickly.

Here are some resources for doing the P-CIP:
Five Rainbows: http://fiverainbows.com/pcip/
CIP Block: http://www.cipblock.com/
The Donohue Group: http://dginc.com/pcip
Casssidy Cataloging: http://cassidycataloguing.com/services/pcip.php

NOTE: All works submitted to the Copyright Office to meet copyright obligations are also reviewed by Library of Congress selection librarians. Works selected for addition to the Library's collections are assigned a cataloging priority and cataloged according to that priority. The Library does NOT provide current status reports for individual works processed in this manner. The Library of Congress database, however, is available via the Internet (http://catalog.loc.gov) and can be searched for works that the Library has cataloged. However, updates to this database can take as long as 18 months.

If your book has already been published, then getting a CIP record is no longer an option. However, you can obtain a MARC record. A MARC record is another way to provide libraries with cataloging data that can perform a similar function to CIP or PCIP data.

A MARC record is a computer file in a specific electronic format designed for library computer systems. Each record contains the same data found in a PCIP data block, plus additional information. Like the PCIP records you can get professionals to create these MARC records. The costs are similar, in the $60-$80 range. Here are some resources for that:

http://fiverainbows.com/marc/
http://www.dginc.com/for-publishers-and-vendors/marc-records/

What *Not* to Include on Your Copyright Page. A "stripped book" statement. This is a statement seen on mass-market paperback fiction.

It is usually at the top of the page and set off in a box. Below is a copy of such a statement.

The sale of this book without its cover is unauthorized. If you purchased the book without a cover, you should be aware that it was reported to the publisher as "unsold and destroyed." Neither the author nor the publisher has received payment for the sale of this "stripped book."

Most self-published books are in trade paperback or hardcover format. These formats are never stripped. Please do not include this on your copyright page unless you have made arrangements with an offset printer to produce mass-market paperback books *and* have made arrangements with booksellers to return them to you stripped for credit. This means those books will no longer be usable for sale.

Author Letter

The author letter is similar to a foreword in that it talks about the book, what to expect, and may include what inspired the author to write the book. It is addressed directly to the reader. This is a common practice in the romance genre. However, I've seen it employed in historical fiction, crime fiction, and in some non-fiction. The primary purpose is to share something with the reader that relates to the content or research of the book.

I used an author letter in a women's fiction novel that included rape recovery as the theme. I wanted readers to be forewarned in case this was an issue that was difficult for them. I also used the letter as a way to draw attention to the problems of rape and how different women react. Author Delilah Marvelle has used author letters in her historical romance fiction as a way to summarize the themes of the story and to express her interest in the research for the era.

Non-fiction authors most often use the author letter to discuss how they undertook the research and why this particular topic was of such importance or interest to the writer. They also use it as a suggestion for how to navigate the content beyond using the table of contents. In memoirs or self-help books, authors will sometimes use the author letter as a means to describe their expectations of the reader when they complete the book.

The author letter is usually placed at the front of the book, before the title page and copyright.

Foreword

Foreword—meaning before the "word" or before the story, the book begins—is always written by someone other than the primary author of the book. It is often written by someone who is prominent in the field (in the case of non-fiction) or a bestselling author in the same genre (in the case of fiction). Sometimes it will be written by an editor, in the case of a collection of stories in an anthology. The narrative typically includes a story of how the foreword author and the book author know each other and why the foreword writer believes this book is worth reading. Later editions of a book sometimes have a new foreword, which appears before an older foreword, if there was one. The new foreword might explain in what respects that edition differs from previous ones.

The primary purpose of a foreword is for marketing. An opening statement by a well-published author gives added credibility, a "stamp of approval" for the book. The foreword tends to appear after the table of contents but before the first chapter of the book.

Table of Contents

In a print book, the table of contents provides a quick index to all of the chapters. This is very important in a non-fiction book where a reader may skip chapters and move forward and backward within the text.

Tip: Both Microsoft Word and Open Office have an automated means for generating a table of contents from headers within the book. See instruction links below for each platform. This can be a real time saver.

Microsoft Word: http://bit.ly/fhVMak
  Open Office: http://bit.ly/JWsHDz

A fiction book rarely has a table of contents. Fiction is usually designed in such a way that the reader must engage with the earlier chapters in order to be caught up with the action and characters in later chapters.

Ebooks for both fiction and non-fiction have a type of table of contents. That is, they provide a linking and bookmarking system for chapters that helps readers to more easily stop and start without losing their place. When the reader returns to the book, she is placed within the chapter last read. It also allows readers to skip to different sections in the ebook.

Most formatting software will automatically generate a table of contents or bookmarking system for your ebooks. If you are creating your files through HTML you will need to manually create these links yourself.

Some fiction does included titled chapters as those often seen in YA and children's fiction. In that situation, a table of contents may be included.

Dedication

This section is where you select a person or group to which you dedicate the book. The narrative tends to be short and personal. Authors frequently dedicate books to family members or friends who were particularly supportive. However, often a book is dedicated to someone who may never read it or may not even be alive. I've seen dedications to English teachers, parents, pets, or even to another author who inspired the writer.

The dedication is different from the acknowledgements section (see Acknowledgments below). The dedication tends to be more inspirational than practical. It is also possible to dedicate the book to someone and include him or her in the acknowledgments. For example, I dedicated my first published book, *Expendable*, to my husband because without his belief in me I would never have finished it. I also mentioned him in the acknowledgments section specifically for his moral support and, because it involved military protocols that he knew and which helped me fashion the story.

Acknowledgements

This section is significantly longer than the dedication and includes all those who had some impact on getting the book completed. It includes practical assistance such as critique partners, beta readers, editors, and other authors who perhaps helped guide the work. It can also include friends and family who offered moral support, did housework during deadlines, or took the kids for a weekend while you recovered.

Similar to the dedication, the acknowledgments are definitely personal. It is up to the author to determine how short or long to make the acknowledgments. However, it is recommended not to exceed two pages. One page is preferred.

When acknowledgments are in the front matter, they typically appear after the dedication. However, in the last three to five years I have more often seen acknowledgments placed in the back matter following the last chapter.

Marketing Related Front Matter

The remaining types of front matter are all marketing-related materials. These are pages designed to convince the reader to buy the book. All of these tend to come before the title page.

A one-page excerpt is used to draw the reader immediately into the story. The excerpt is rarely from the first page. Instead select an excerpt that provides good "reader cookies." This is usually a section with action or conflict that is typical of the genre. For example, a romance excerpt might be a first kiss or a lead-up to sexual tension. In a thriller or suspense novel, the excerpt will be an action scene where the protagonist is put in jeopardy. The excerpt may come from any part of the book, but should not reveal a major turning point or the climax of the story.

Praise or pull quotes from advanced reviews are also used to convince the browsing reader to purchase the book. If this is the first book by the author, it helps to get some advanced reviews and include them in the front of the book. If it is a second or third book, you can also use the reviews from a previous book to draw readers in. This is particularly true if the second book is part of the same series.

When using advance praise, it is most helpful to get quotes from well-known authors in the same genre. In the case of non-fiction, getting quotes or reviews from experts in the field or other authors who have written on the same topic is critical. The key to using these quotes is not to provide an entire review, but to pick out parts of the quote that are most likely to pull in a reader. Adjectives like top-notch, fast-paced, true-to-life, and insightful are all good ones for fiction. For non-fiction, look for quotes with words like comprehensive, practical, applicable, and invaluable. Of course, any words that capture the nature of the book and the excitement in reading it are great to have.

The final type of marketing front matter that is often included is a listing of other books by the author. Depending on the purpose, some writers prefer to put this listing at the back of the book instead of the front. The decision whether this should be front matter or back matter has to do with where you are in your writing career.

In fiction, if you are a fairly new author—perhaps with only two or three books—it might be advantageous to have them at the front. This alerts potential buyers or reviewers that you are not a one-book author. Also, if the book is part of a series, it helps to have the entire series listed at the front of the book. In this way, the potential buyer immediately knows that perhaps she should go back and get the previous books first to make she enters the series with full knowledge of the characters and the world set up.

If you have written many books, or books that are unrelated to each other, consider moving this section to back matter.

The question to ask yourself in making decisions about all the marketing front matter is: If a reader is finding my books for the first time, what will most impress him or her about me and this book? The answer will help you decide where to place your book list and other materials.

Chapter Four
BACK MATTER

Back matter is all of the materials that come after the end of the narrative. As discussed in the previous section, an author may choose to place some typical front matter text in the back. Some things to include in the back matter that I've already discussed are acknowledgments and a list of other books by the author.

The primary purpose of the back matter is to get readers to purchase another book by the author or the publisher. It does this by focusing on two areas: marketing additional books by the author; and convincing readers to learn more by signing up to receive newsletters or emails about upcoming books. Let's look at each of these techniques. Whether you have only one book or many books, both of these techniques can increase your future sales.

Marketing Additional Books by the Author

Previously, I've discussed providing a listing of additional books. For a print book, it is helpful to provide a list divided by genre and series relationships. With an ebook, you can provide a link directly to where the reader can buy each book. It is easiest if those links are on your website so you can provide a single link for each book that has all the vendors who distribute your books.

If you only have a few books to offer, you may wish to include a very brief description for each book (three to four lines) along with a thumbnail cover to entice readers to try them. If you have more than three or four books, a simple listing of the books is sufficient. If the book that has just been completed is part of a series, you definitely want to include all other books in the series as part of your list—including unpublished titles if you know the titles and approximate release dates.

Another very popular tool to tempt readers to buy the next book is to offer a "sneak preview" by providing an excerpt or the entire first chapter along with a link to that book page so they can easily click and buy it before putting your current book down.

This is particularly important if you are doing a series and something difficult or horrible has happened to the main character at the end of your book. You want readers to know that in the next book, either the main character or those close to her will be looking to resolve the problem. Even if the next book isn't finished, it helps to provide this first chapter to let readers know it is scheduled and coming soon.

If you don't have another book to offer or your other books are in a different genre with a different reading audience, consider partnering with another author to exchange "sneak peeks." Perhaps you know someone who writes dragon stories similar to yours. You can feature the first chapter from one of her books in exchange for her featuring the first chapter from one of your books. You both win and you've already begun some cross promoting and marketing together.

When I wrote my *DIY Publishing* book, my fiction titles did not serve as good preview candidates for a non-fiction book on indie publishing. Furthermore, my previously published non-fiction books about technology and distance learning did not have the same audience as DIY Publishing book. So, I partnered with author Jamie Brazil and her non-fiction book geared to newer writers. Her focus included both traditional and indie suggestions for getting a new book out to readers.

We both featured first chapter excerpts of our non-fiction books in the "sneak peak" back matter of our books.

Getting the Reader Invested in Learning More

Two things that every writer needs to gain sales are reviews of the book and readers who wish to learn about upcoming books. Reviews helps readers who are browsing determine what other readers liked or disliked about your book. Inviting readers to join a mailing list provides you with a built-in means of providing information every time you publish. The best way to get both of these is to ask for it.

At the back of every one of my books, print and ebook, I do two things: I ask readers to consider leaving a review and I ask them to sign up for my mailing list. In the ebooks I provide a clickable link to my mailing list.

Let me share with you ideas about how to make these requests. I present both requests on the same page. These requests are positioned on the page following the end of the narrative and before any other back matter. When a reader finishes your book and feels satisfied, it is the best time to get him or her to act. The best way to determine exactly what you want to say is to read several examples from other authors and determine what fits your voice and style. Below is mine. Feel free to use my words, or some variation, in your own books.

Example at the back of each book in my YA Fantasy series.

New Release Mailing List

Want to find out what happens next to Camryn and the rest of the forest people? Sign up for my mailing list *http://maggiefaire.com/mailing-list.html* to be the first to know when the next book comes out. I do not spam anybody and I do not release your name or email to anyone else. You only receive an email when the next book is within one month of availability. Also, any pre-release deals or special sales for the books will go first to those on the mailing list.

Consider Writing a Review

Word-of-mouth is crucial for any author to succeed. If you enjoyed the book, please consider leaving a review on GoodReads and on the retailer site where you purchased the book (e.g., Amazon, Kobo, Apple, B&N). If you are a librarian and subscribe to LibraryThing or Shelfari, please also consider leaving a review there. Even if it were only a line or two, it would make all the difference and would be very much appreciated.

Example of request from Jamie Brazil's YA Historical Fiction, *The Commodore's Daughter.*

I can't give you permission to use this one because it definitely reflects her personality and style. It is also specific to this book. However, I wanted to offer it as an example of how you can insert your own voice into your requests.

And now, a personal appeal from Jamie:

Thank you for reading The Commodore's Daughter. I hope you enjoyed the story as much as I enjoyed writing it. Commodore Perry's journey of 1853 has been widely documented. There are genealogical accounts of the Commodore's wife and daughter, Caroline. However, Caroline did not have a sibling. While this novel has elements of a historical event that dramatically transformed two countries, Jennifer Perry is a fictional character.

She was also a labor of love. This novel took over five years to complete. And I swore to never write another historic novel again...

except... well... I'm fascinated with the past and history has a way of seeping into my brain and leaking out my fingertips. In flawed, but perhaps interesting ways.

You be the judge. Which is what I'm asking you to do.

Strike asking. How about begging? Please, please, please share your thoughts in the form of a review. Reader reviews are the engine of independent publishing, and your opinion – whether you loved this novel or hated it – helps shape the future for digital books and indie authors like myself.

The future is at your fingertips. Please share your thoughts!

Sincerely,

Jamie Brazil

Example of providing incentive for a review instead of a direct request.

Please tell other readers why you liked this book by reviewing it at one of the following websites: Amazon, Barnes and Noble, Kobo, Apple or Goodreads. If you do write a review, please send an email to author @gmail.com. I would like to gift you a copy of the next book in the series as a way of thanking you.

UPDATE: Since I combined all my pseudonyms and genres into one website, I've given up on tracking multiple pseudonyms on separate mailing lists and separate sites. I now refer everyone to my website where I offer free books in each genre as one way to get on my mailing list OR I have a menu item on my site called Mailing Lists. There I maintain links to the types of list I maintain by genre and a general list for everything. In that way I can change mail providers or add/subtract genres without having to update all my links in all my books.

I use an email list provider who allows me to tag a variety of mail list types and keep them in one big list with the ability to select a segment as needed. If you write in more than one genre you might want to consider this. Though I have decent cross-over in my romance subgenres, and a little between romance readers and my SF/Fantasy fans, there are definitely a number of readers who do NOT want to get information about a genre they don't read.

Other Back Matter

Book lists, sneak previews, and requests for readers to do reviews and join mailing lists all meet the criteria for using marketing in back matter. There is also back matter that relates to the book itself and helps the reader to engage or learn more about the story or to use a non-fiction book more effectively. Those things would be:

- Index - Only used in non-fiction, the index provides an easy way to find terms in the main body of the text. It is a type of navigation guide to the book.
- Glossary – For fiction, this might contain foreign words or phrases used in the story. For non-fiction, it would contain specialty jargon relating to the content (e.g., a list of computer terms).
- Maps of relevant areas.
- Links to additional references or more information.
- Afterword – Similar to a foreword, the afterword explores how the book came to be written or how the ideas were developed. The book's primary author writes it. In later editions, the afterword might be written by a well-respected individual who comments on the book's impact.
- Appendix – Only used in non-fiction, it provides supplementary materials to the book that usually add details, tables, raw data, or updates and corrections to earlier material.
- Bibliography or Reference List – Primarily used in non-fiction books that are research intensive. Memoirs, self-help, or opinion pieces that attempt to consolidate "common knowledge" on a subject rarely contain a

bibliography, though they may contain footnotes or links to additional information.

Finally, you should always include links to your website, blog, and social media. If you have a publishing company and a site that represents your books, you should include that on the final page of the book.

Chapter Five
COVER DESIGN

An attractive cover can convince someone to buy your book without knowing anything more than the genre. A bad cover will just as surely cause a potential buyer to turn away from all your hard work. I am the first to admit that I do not prepare my own covers. I learned early on that just because I have a good eye for selecting images and know my way around Photoshop does not mean I can create an eye-catching and effective cover. It is more than technique and more than "I'll know it when I see it." It is art; and because covers are so critical to sales, I've chosen to always have a professional cover designer create mine.

However, even if you hire a cover designer, it still helps to understand what makes a good cover. A designer will ask what you want, ask you to point to covers you like, and may ask you to send stock image comps for her to use in your cover.

Cover design consists of marrying image, color, and typography in a way that not only captures the reader's attention but also conveys the genre and story theme. That is a lot to accomplish! So, what is it that makes a great cover? I've narrowed it down to four important first-impression items.

1. It looks professional. In other words, it looks like something NY would put out.
2. It fits genre expectations.
3. The author's name is easy to read, even in thumbnail view at only 150 pixels tall.
4. The title is easy to read and the typography is indicative of the genre.

Let me share a few of my own covers and talk about what works and what doesn't. I've learned this over the past five years and I hope to save you some of that trial and error.

First the good. My cover for *Chameleon: The Awakening* (YA Urban Fantasy) has drawn in readers beginning with my first cover reveal several months before the book was available. It is the only one of my book covers that booksellers, readers, and other authors always tell me they love. Many reviews of the book have begun with "I was drawn in by the cover."

After my first book signing for this series, the bookseller loved the cover so much she had it made into a giant poster that hung in the front window in order to intrigue buyers to come into the store.

Of all the covers I have loaded on Pinterest, this cover gets the most interest and re-pins. In short, having a great cover will get you exposure in a lot more places than in an online catalog. Is it surprising that this book has done better than any other so far?

What works with this cover? First it has a central image that is appealing. Most YA fantasy and paranormal books feature the protagonist as the central image, so this meets the genre expectations. The typography says "fantasy book." The title and author's name are all easy to read. The series' title is also clear. In other words, it hits all the reader cookies.

Now let's look at a not-so-successful cover and its replacement to understand what went wrong.

Looks gorgeous, doesn't it? A graphic artist professionally created it and it has all the elements I asked for. When I received it, I immediately fell in love with the composition, colors and "feeling" of the image. However, I now know there are two major problems and a minor problem with the cover: 1) This is a romance and the romance genre expects a couple on the cover. I only have the protagonist. 2) The author's name and the series name are too small. In thumbnail you can't read the author's name at all. 3) It is too dark. This is not the artist's fault. She was following my rules. However, contemporary romance readers expect lighter backgrounds. Now, let's look at the revised cover. It also proves the point that just because someone is a graphic artist or a Photoshop guru, it doesn't mean he is a cover designer.

A good cover designer understands genre expectations, keeps on top of changes in styles, fonts, colors from year to year for each genre. A good cover designer understands author and series branding, and looks at your work as something that needs to last a long time. Let's face it; you don't want to be changing your cover every year. You need a design that will last a while.

Below is the redesigned cover in 2014. The image of the protagonist is the same, but now the male romantic interest is there as well. My name is easily seen and the series name has been moved to the center of the page. Though there is still a lot of black in it, the cover feels lighter because of the window and the blue-sky background. Also, the use of the window grounds the primary image in a room instead of floating in front of the water. In the thumbnail all the important elements can be seen and read.

The best way to understand covers is to go to a large bookstore or surf online at publisher sites. Do a search on the genre where you believe your book fits and look at the top selling novels (25-50). See what patterns you can define. A good example is YA paranormal books. They almost always have a single teen as the focus of the cover. In contrast, middle-grade paranormal books almost always have an animal or magical person/creature as the focus of the cover. Very different approaches.

Women's fiction may not have a person on the cover at all. It may be a place instead—the beach, a town, a house, or even a simple bouquet of flowers. If there is a person, it tends to be a woman alone, often without her face showing.

A Suspense or a Thriller cover needs to be ominous and dark. Most suspense protagonists are often depicted in silhouette or in shadow. Suspense novels that revolve around a certain type of protagonist (e.g., police, fireman, military) will feature that person or his/her tools like a gun, a badge, a uniform. Note that all these covers don't try to tell the story. Instead they hint at the genre and the theme.

Historical novels have a definite sense of the period—castles, period dress, and antique items feature regularly on covers. Literary novels tend to be all over the map. Science Fiction novels must indicate the science part of the novel on the cover. Space ships, robots, and computers are all popular cover elements.

Non-fiction also has genre types. Memoirs echo much of women's fiction covers—places or single individual pictures. Self-help books are light or saturated with primary colors designed to make the reader feel confident and positive. Non-fiction tends to stress a single image or frequently uses just words and color.

A mistake authors often make is to try to recreate a particular scene on the cover. The difficulty with this approach is that the scene can quickly get busy and there is no room for the author's name, the title, or other details that need to stand out.

Similar to the important one-scene mistake, authors try to capture the entire plot of the book on the cover. For example, I knew an author writing a mystery set in the 1920's. As part of unraveling the mystery the protagonist had to find a special candle, was stabbed by the bad guy, and ended up in a cobblestone alley. She wanted the protagonist dressed as a flapper, slumped in the alley with her pearls, candle, and a knife in a circle around her. Though it meant a lot to the author, the reader picking up the book wouldn't have a relationship to all the objects. Once again it becomes too busy. Selecting the same cobblestone street with only a bloody high heel surrounded by pearls could still invoke the sense of history and danger that the author wants while leaving much more space for typography and focus.

Frequently, the best image is the simplest image with one central focal point. The concept is not to depict scenes, but rather to capture a feeling. Look at covers that draw you in and write down what feeling you get when you view that cover. Then consider how your cover can represent something similar and yet relate to your unique story.

A great resource for studying cover design is the monthly book cover design awards at Joel Friedlander's site.

http://www.thebookdesigner.com/2013/09/e-book-cover-design-awards-august-2013/

Each month he takes 50-80 covers that are submitted by independent authors and designers. He comments on what works and what doesn't. Every time I look at his site, I realize how important it is for the typography and image to work together and I count my blessings that I have a good cover designer who understand my genres.

Branding

The primary purpose of your cover is to sell more books. Assuming you understand the genre expectations, the next thing to consider is branding. There are three elements to consider in cover branding—author, genre, and series. If you only write in one genre you are in an easier branding situation than authors who write in multiple genres like me.

Writers never know what is going to hit first in branding. For some authors it is their series. They begin a series and somewhere around book three it starts to take off. That is a brand to capitalize on. Branding a series involves more than using the series title somewhere on the book, it also requires using the same look and feel for every book in the series. You want readers to immediately recognize your book while flying through online catalogs or review sites. It needs to stand on its own and shout, "This is your series!" before they see the title or the author's name.

My YA Fantasy series is about "the forest people." Therefore I've made the choice that every book will have a background that includes green forest or moss. Lichen plays a major role throughout the series, so it is also on every cover in some way (usually on the protagonist). I am using the name "Chameleon" in every title to help readers immediately connect with the series. They may not remember every book title, but they will know the primary character is a human chameleon. You already saw the font I use. It is distinctive. I'm sure someone else has used that font on a book, but it's not one I see often on fantasy and paranormal titles. All of these elements are series branding.

Author branding on a cover is also achieved through distinct typography. Are you known as an author who writes "dark" narratives or "light" homespun stories? It makes a difference in how your readers perceive you and find your books. The typography for your name needs to reflect that brand from one book to the next. Again, writing only in one genre simplifies matters. If you are writing in two or three genres, consider a typography that is cross-genre for your name.

The CAP Rule—Contrast, Alignment, Proximity

Okay, I admit I made up the acronym CAP. I like mnemonics that help me remember principles. Stacie Vander Pol, owner of Cover Design Studio, talks the "rule of thirds" and the "golden triangle" in graphic design. I was never trained as a graphic designer, so I highly recommend reading her two part tutorial on cover design at her website. http://www.coverdesignstudio.com/layout-rule-of-thirds-diagonal-scan-and-more/

Stacie also provides two well-organized YouTube tutorials for designing your cover using Gimp and Photoshop Elements.

Gimp http://www.youtube.com/watch?v=CONohk1H684
Photoshop Elements
http://www.youtube.com/watch?v=YZ307Z02aLM

I will summarize her "rule of thirds" and how I believe it also illustrates the CAP rule. Stacie states that elements on the page should be divided into thirds, either horizontally or vertically. This makes the image more appealing and fits the **alignment** part of the CAP rule. The center third is the focal point and thus usually where the highest **contrast** occurs—where you want the eye to look first. The horizon of the image should appear in the upper or lower third rather than straight through the middle. This relates to the **proximity** part of CAP.

The Western eye views images from the top left to the bottom right. Composing the image and typography to take advantage of this comfort zone feels "right" to buyers.

Below is an example of a simple but eye-catching cover from William Hertling that uses the rule of thirds well. Consider whether this meets the expectations of his SF readers.

Proximity places the central image—the banks of servers—in the center third of the page. Alignment places the title in the upper third and the author name in the lower third. The contrast of the red typography with the black and white picture not only makes the title and author name stand out, but also frames the central image while suggesting the possibility of fear and destruction. Placing the helicopter in the top left helps the eye track from left to right and balances the slightly off-center diminishing horizon in the primary image. The only thing I would suggest changing on this cover is to make the author's name larger. I suspect that in thumbnail, his name is unreadable.

I don't know if William Hertling did the cover himself or not. I do know it is a self-published title that has done well in the market. The image, titling, and typography also match the science fiction genre in which he writes.

Typography

The title, author name and series title are absolute musts for all books. In addition, you may wish to include tags—a descriptor or modifier to the title or author's name. The key is not to use every bit of space on the cover. The eye needs rest. If the tags overwhelm the central focus, the cover appears busy and distracting. On the other hand, tags can make great points and help readers make the decision to buy.

Bestselling authors (i.e., USA Today or New York Times Bestselling Author) definitely want to include that tag on every cover. The placement should be near your name—either above or below. Tags should be identified with the part of the typography it modifies. Your bestselling status is part of your author brand.

I have seen many books that simply have "Bestselling Author" or "Award Winning Author" as the tag on the cover. Carefully consider what that says to readers. The fact that the bestselling or award winning status is not defined is a red flag to many readers. Unfortunately, too many independent authors have been putting those undefined tags on books in an attempt to compete more effectively. All it takes is one or two readers to research your claim and if it turns our your award was for an unpublished manuscript or a paid position on a small list your reputation is sullied.

If you have won a major published book award in your genre, by all means say so. RITA Award Winner does garner respect from romance readers. Hugo Award Winner is important to science fiction readers. Winning an Edgar or Agatha in mystery is also something worthy of putting on the front cover.

However, if your award was won in a contest where you submitted three chapters prior to publication, I'm not sure that is the best use of your brand. Certainly, you should be proud of it. But save those types of awards for your author biography.

The same reasoning applies to tagging yourself as "Bestselling Author" on the cover. If you aren't willing to state how or where you are a bestseller it should not be on the cover. Again, readers are wary of this title. It seems that every indie author is a bestseller somewhere which makes the tag useless if it isn't associated with a known list like USA Today, New York Times, or Publishers Weekly. Being in the Amazon Top 100 when you put your book up for free downloads does not count. Being a bestseller at a small press where bestselling means you sold thirty books in one month or even 100 is not worth the possibility of tainting your author brand.

What if you are an Amazon bestseller or a Barnes & Noble bestseller on the paid list? Honestly, I'm not sure how that works as an author tag. Personally, I would consider using that as part of my excerpts and quotes in the front of the book rather than on the cover. Of course, it is up to you what to put on your book. Just remember the trade offs and possible consequences.

You don't have to have "Bestselling Author" or "Award Winning Author" on your cover to sell books. In fact, literary awards and bestseller status is far down readers' lists of how they find you or choose to take a chance on you. In Reader surveys, readers identify they find new authors first because of an interesting cover, then by reading a good blurb, and finally by being drawn into an excerpt or viewing the first chapter. Seeing "Bestselling Author" on the cover falls somewhere around number nine on a list of top ten items.

Be proud of who you are as a published author and confident in what you write. Let your name and the work speak for itself. Don't allow desperation for sales now create false impressions of your author brand that will haunt you in the future. If your cover is inviting and the book is interesting, it will find a readership. Your popularity will build. When you win a major literary award or make a major bestseller list is the time to make it part of your author brand and tag the cover.

Another tag often used on covers is a pull quote or short review blurb. This type of tag should be placed near the title. In this case, a quote or blurb is modifying a particular work. Pull quotes work best when they are from a major reviewer or a bestselling author in your genre. If your quotes do not meet that criterion, leave them off the cover. Instead, use them in the interior as part of the front matter.

Below are two covers that use all of these tags while maintaining author, genre, and series branding.

Note that both authors have their bestselling tags near their name. In Fyffe's instance, she has placed it above her name. Naughton put the tag below her name. Both work because the placement is in a section of the image that is not too busy. These novels are part of a series and the series branding is obvious. The McCutcheon Family books all have the small badge at the bottom in Fyffe's series. The Eternal Guardians novels always display the omega symbol and the name inside as a series tag.

Both authors also have pull quotes on the cover. On *Montana Dawn,* the quote is more centered, instead of pulled closer to the title. On *Marked,* the quote is obviously tagged to the large title. Finally, on both covers the title and author names are easy to read at this size and at thumbnail size.

One more possibility is to use a "tag line" that represents the book or series instead of a pull quote. Below is another example from Elisabeth Naughton. Above the title she has placed a tag line to capture the essence of the story arc. It reads: "He lost her once. He won't lose her again." Along with the cover images, which meet romance genre expectations, good typography on the title and author name, this short tag line adds one more draw to move a potential reader toward a buy decision. It must have worked. *Wait for Me* was Elisabeth's first book to make the New York Times Bestseller List. It stayed at number one and two for a long time.

Selecting Art

Few writers are photographers or artists. This means that it is most likely you will be using licensed photography, also known as "stock photography." There are many stock photography sites. The key is to find one or two that seem to meet most of your needs. Below are the ones I'm personally familiar with using.

iStockphoto http://www.istockphoto.com/
   Fotolia http://us.fotolia.com/
   Dreamstime http://www.dreamstime.com/
   Getty Images http://www.gettyimages.com

Most sites require you to pre-purchase "credits." These are usually sold as one dollar equals one credit. The cost per credit decreases with the more credits you purchase. Because of this you want to be sure that whatever site you choose is one that is likely to have many images you can use. Images include photographs, original artwork, videos and vector art.

Be cautious when using art from a non-stock site. For example, many authors may fall in love with a particular piece of original art from a site like Deviant Art. It has certainly happened to me. The difficulty with sites like that is that they are set up primarily as a portfolio showcase for the artist. They are not set up as an ecommerce site, nor does it have standard licensing. This means the author must negotiate with each artist separately. Some of the artists are familiar with licensing and have contracts ready to go while others do not, which leaves the onus on you. Furthermore, artists may leave art up for long periods of time but be virtually unreachable, as they haven't checked into the site for years.

The key to finding stock images that meet your needs is using search terms at these sites. In addition to searching by descriptions (e.g., female, brunette), also search by moods (e.g., sad, happy, pensive) and by locations (e.g., Scotland, Maine, New Zealand, urban, rural).

Once you have located something that is close, also search the artist's portfolio. You can usually do this by clicking on the artist's name. Some sites also have a link titled "more of this model" or something similar. This means it will look for additional images that were part of the same photo shoot, as well as pictures of the same model.

It is easy to fixate on a particular model because he or she matches the character in your mind. For me, that often happens on some of the more expensive images. Because my budget is limited, I always look for model images that are under $5 for the size I need. On special occasions I might go as high as $10. I'm not willing to pay $50 or $100 because I like to keep my per book costs down as much as possible and I know my cover designer will make the model into what I need. Your budget and choices may be different.

Consider partial images. Though it is wonderful to find a single image you love, often covers are made up of two or three images blended together. Also remember, if you are working with a cover designer, or have the skills yourself, things like hair color and eye color can be changed. Skin tones can be lightened or darkened, and a certain amount of clothing can be added or modified. In other words look for the big ideas.

Once you have selected images, download the comps. These are images that are smaller and tend to be watermarked with a copyright symbol or the photo distributor name in it. The purpose is for you to play with them and see if they will really work for you. Ignore the distracting watermark and mock-up a cover, by placing the images in the positions and proportions you were considering. Once you are sure the images do what you need, go back and pay for the appropriate license.

For example, on my cover for *Chameleon: The Choosing*, I provided three different images to the cover designer. One was an image of a cave with a waterfall. There were people in the cave and outside. Another was an image of a girl walking in a forest of brown trees. The third was an image of a young man lying face down in a grassy water area. The cover designer was able to take the individual images and manipulate them, then blend them on the cover into a single image. This takes time, skill, and talent. If you don't have these skills or time, contract with a professional.

Below, see thumbnails of the original three images given to the cover designer, and then the finished product. Total cost to purchase the stock images from iStockphoto was 23 credits. Because I had previously purchased a large batch of credits on sale, the actual cost for me was $12.00 for all three images.

In the first image, notice that the model is walking in a brown forest and is facing in a different direction. On the final cover design, the designer increased the hair color to be a more vibrant red and changed the eye color to be blue. The hair and eye detail matches the model in the first book of the series, even though we did not use the same model. The designer also changed the direction the model faced and placed her in the cave. She added lichen growing on her arm, which is a feature of the protagonist in each book. Lichen gives the forest people special magical powers.

In the second photo, the male model is in a very different environment than the cave where he was placed on the cover. The stock photo shows him in a flooded grassy and the full nude body is exposed. In the cover, the lower half of the body is covered in moss and the model is placed on a slope. Also, like the protagonist, lichen was added to his body.

A good cover designer can take parts of photos and manipulate them to fit the needs of your novel. You do not have to find the exact model in the exact location that matches your novels story. Models can be cut out and put elsewhere, images reversed, hair color changed, clothing added or taken away to a certain extent, clothing colors changed, skin color lightened or darkened. In the same way a makeup artist for movies can create a different creature or make an actor look unrecognizable, so can I good cover artist.

The cave image above is the primary background photo for the cover. Though it is hard to see in this thumbnail, there were people hiking both inside and outside the cave that needed to be removed. In addition, the cover designer added more moss throughout the picture and darkened the clouds and sky to increase the ominous mood I wanted to portray. The completed cover design is below.

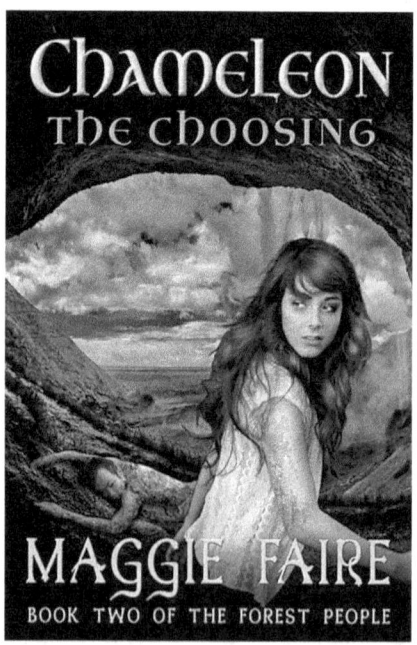

Though your cover may not be as complex as this one, I hope this example helps you to see that an image does not have to be perfect when you purchase it. It needs to be close to expressing the idea you want to convey. With photo manipulation, highlights, contrasts, and color changes the cover can become unique, eye-catching, and meet your needs with a little work.

Free Stock Photos are available. A good site with a list of these is Bookstrap Bay https://bootstrapbay.com/blog/free-stock-photos/

Something to watch for when looking at free stock photo sites is the sizing. For a print book cover, all images need to be 300dpi or more. Some free photos are small or not very many pixels because they were taken with a phone or an older camera. However, many of them are quite professional. Also, on free sites you want to be sure that the license does allow you to use the photos in commercial work.

Stock Photo Licensing

Be sure to read the licenses associated with the photos you wish to use. You pay by the size of the photo and the license type on the photo. Remember, that for print books you need 300 dpi quality. This usually means you need files that are approximately 2200 pixels on the long side. In most stock photo purchase sites this file size is labeled "large" or "extra large."

For images to be used only for ebooks, 72 to 150 dpi will be sufficient for most displays. However, you do need to worry about the requirements at each vendor. It seems that size standards increase every year or two as tablet and ereader technology advances. Amazon is now requiring 1200 pixels with 2100 pixels on the long side preferred. I would go for the largest size you can afford.

When you evaluate licenses, look for the following items and make sure they are covered to meet your needs.

- **Time Limits** – What is the cost and what does that buy you? You want to make sure you can use that image in perpetuity. A time-limited license (i.e., 2 years) is not helpful when it is likely your book will be available for decades.
- **Use Limits** – Does the license only allow you to use it on your

cover? What if you want to put the cover on your website or use it in a marketing campaign? Make sure the license allows that. Sometimes you will have to pay more for that privilege.
- ***Model Release*** – Does the license include a release from the model and what does that entail? Most licenses do include model releases of some type. However, some models include restrictions on the use of the image. For example, the model cannot be clothed in certain types of outfits or posed within certain scenarios. Most of these restrictions are sexual in nature. If you are looking for sexy poses for your book be sure to select models who are already posed in that manner in the original image. Their release will likely be unrestricted for that type of use.

Though stock photo licenses can contain a variety of restrictions, most sites have three types of licenses available: royalty-free, rights-managed, and extended. The royalty free license is the most common and affordable. I always look for those licenses first. Some sites call this royalty free license "standard license."

Royalty-Free License. Royalty free means you can use the image multiple times, without paying a royalty. The downside of royalty free is that the images are non-exclusive, meaning anyone can purchase and use them. This sometimes results in seeing a particular image (particularly some popular models) on lots of book covers (e.g., a man and woman kissing). When choosing a royalty free image, you may wish to scan a number of book covers in your genre and make sure that particular image is not being used on very many of them.

Because all of my book covers use only parts of images and often change them significantly (e.g., hair color, location, clothing), I never purchase an exclusive license. The book cover with a variety of art becomes a separate image that is unique. Unless you are using a single image for your cover, and it is important to be exclusive, I don't recommend paying for exclusivity. Exclusivity costs hundreds and often thousands of dollars. Royalty free images are often as little as $2 to $5 and have the most lenient permissible uses for both commercial and personal projects.

On the other hand, if you are planning a series of books and want to be sure the same model is available for all of them, you might consider working with a professional photographer and doing an actual photo shoot. If you are a professional photographer this is a great way to get exclusive photos. If you are paying a photographer, this may cost you $300 to $500, depending on time and model fees. Amortized over many books in a series, it may be worthwhile in the end. It all depends on your budget and how important exclusivity and having the same model are to you.

Rights-Managed License. A rights-managed license offers exclusive, time-limited use of a stock image. This will cost more than the royalty free license. The license is granted on a pay-per-use basis. That means the image can only be used for one particular project *and* for a set period of time. Some licenses are specific to a geographic area (i.e., only in Oregon or only in the United States). This type of license is rarely used for book covers. It is more often used for a specific marketing campaign.

Extended or Enhanced License. An extended or enhanced license is usually a license that "extends" permissions for a royalty free license. For example, most royalty free licenses allow you to use the image in many venues—on your cover, on your website, in marketing campaigns, etc. However, they do not allow you to resell the image in other products, such as on a calendar, t-shirts, greeting cards, or a print-on-demand image of your primary character. If you anticipate selling the royalty free images beyond the use in your book cover, then you will need the Extended or Enhanced License.

In most cases, you can purchase a standard license and if your needs change, return and purchase a different license to meet upgraded needs. This is more costly than purchasing the correct license the first time. However, if you are unsure of your use beyond the book cover, I suggest purchasing the license that best meets your immediate needs. That is the least expensive option.

NOTE: Most cover designers have stock photo providers they know well and include some number of photos or a budget for photos within their design costs. If you decide to work with a designer, ask about how they source photos and what costs are passed to you.

Aspect Ratios

Another important part of cover design is the concept of aspect ratio of the finished design. Print books and ebooks have slightly different preferences. A professional cover designer understands this and therefore gives you different cover aspect ratios for print and ebooks.

What is an aspect ratio? It is a graphic term that describes the relative horizontal and vertical sizes. For example, if a graphic has an aspect ratio of 2:1, it means that the width is twice as large as the height. When resizing graphics, it is important to maintain the aspect ratio to avoid stretching the graphic out of proportion. Books tend to be significantly taller than wide. For example a book designed for a 6" x 9" trim size would have an aspect ratio of 1:1.5. In other words the height is 1.5 times the width. A different trim size selection would have a different aspect ratio.

Ebooks tend to follow a similar aspect ratio design. Some vendors definitely recommend a 1:1.5 aspect ratio or a 2:3 aspect ratio, while others simply list pixel minimums for the longest side. So what does that mean when the recommendation is to go above 2,000 pixels on the longest side? Below are three typical sizing possibilities that match this 1:1.5 or 2:3 aspect ratio.

- 1400 x 2100
- 1667 x 2500

- 2500 x 3750

You don't have to do these calculations yourself. Most graphics programs have the ability to expand or reduce the size of the graphic while maintaining the proportion.

Whenever given a choice, it is best to go with the largest size possible. As computers, tablets, and e-readers become more high definition vendors expect more definition in your covers as well. Currently the minimum size is the 1400 x 2100. Apple and Amazon prefer the 2500 x 3750.

Working With a Cover Designer

If you are like me, either your design skills or time availability are limited. Like writers and editors, cover designers come at a variety of costs and skill levels. When looking for a cover designer I suggest doing the following.

1. Look at books that have a cover style you like. Go to the copyright page and see if the cover designer is listed. If not there, go to the acknowledgments.
2. Ask your author friends who they use and what the relationship is like.
3. Type "cover design" into a search engine and a number of companies will come up.
4. Go to the designer sites you are considering and look at their portfolios. It is important to evaluate whether all their books look good or only a few. Even bad designers get lucky once in a while because a particular customer is very knowledgeable. But good designers will have many great covers and will display them in their portfolio.
5. Make sure the designer has created covers in your genre. Understanding the reader expectations for a genre is critical in a cover design. A science fiction cover designer may not do a good job on a romance. A designer who primarily

works in non-fiction may not understand the expectations of genre fiction.
6. Look at the costs and determine if they are within your budget. Costs typically range from $100 to over $1,000. You can get a good design for between $100 and $300 if you are careful whom you choose. The higher-cost designers tend to be people with decades of experience and a reputation in publishing. If you need something unique and have the budget and time, a higher-cost designer may work well for you.

Once you have selected a designer, make an appointment to speak with him or her on the phone. It is important to get a feel for how your relationship will work and if you feel comfortable asking questions. You also want someone who is confident and experienced enough to be honest about the viability of your cover ideas. If the designer believes your cover vision will not provide the most effective marketing, he or she should be able to explain the reasons the cover won't work and offer alternatives. You do not want a designer who will implement your cover vision knowing that it will be ineffective.

Here are some questions to consider asking the designer during your telephone, email, or in-person interview.

1. How many covers have you designed in my genre?
2. What do you believe must be included on my cover to meet genre expectations?
3. What is your typical timeline for a design project? Are there additional fees if I need it sooner than that?
4. What is your preferred communication? Phone, email, text message?
5. How many mock-ups do you provide?
6. How many changes are allowed with the standard pricing?
7. Do you pay for the stock photos or do I?

8. What type of information do I need to provide about my book and what I see as the cover?
9. Is there a discount for multiple books, such as a series? If so, do the books need to be contracted within a specific period of time to obtain the discount?
10. If we disagree about what to include on the cover, what will be the result?
11. If I cannot accept the final design, is there still a cost I'm obligated to pay?
12. Assuming we both love the cover, will you be including my cover in your portfolio?

Once you have established a relationship and a timeline, it is important to articulate your vision for the book both in words and images. Many designers will ask you to send them pictures of book covers you like and that reflect your expectations for the look and feel of your book. This helps them get an idea of your taste. Some designers will also ask what colors you see as important to the book. Remember, this is not necessarily your favorite colors but the colors that will meet genre expectations.

Nearly all designers will ask for a summary of your book. Your back cover blurb or the blurb you put up for an ebook provides this information. Some designers will go further and also ask for you to describe your main character(s) in terms of gender, age, hair color, eye color, etc. This helps them to look for stock photos and models that may come close.

I've found that if I have a clear vision for the book cover, it helps to provide specific stock photo images to the designer. Again, no need to purchase them yet. Simply send the comps. As I detailed earlier in how the *Chameleon: The Choosing* book came together, I found the images and sent them to the designer with a description of what I envisioned. In this way, the designer is not spending time looking for images that I will ultimately not like because it doesn't fit what is in my mind.

I do not always have such a clear vision. On a different cover, the third book in my Sweetwater Canyon romance series, I was not as clear. I knew I wanted a couple on the cover because it was a romance. I also knew it needed to be in the country and my protagonist would be playing the guitar. Other than that I did not have an idea of the composition or what the character needed to look like. In that instance, I sent three model comps of the female protagonist and two model comps of the male along with several possible background comps. I left it up to the designer to determine which things went together most effectively.

If you don't have any idea what you want, then a written description is sufficient. However, your description needs to communicate more than plot. Be sure to describe the mood, tone, and themes of your book as much as possible. Then keep an open mind to what the designer presents. It is unfair to say, "I don't have any idea what I want" and then get upset because the designer didn't give you what you secretly had in mind.

Even when you have a clear vision and provide all the images, you need to still be open to suggestion. Remember, the reason you are hiring a cover designer is because you don't have the expertise or time to do it yourself. This means the designer may present things in a way you didn't expect. This is because she understands proportion, typography, focus, and genre. You need to listen to the reasons she made those choices and carefully consider them.

Whenever you get a draft design or several mock-ups back, do not immediately accept or reject them. Take a day or two to live with them. If you are unsure, ask trusted author friends to look at them and give you an opinion. Sometimes a cover that rubs you the wrong way might be exactly what you need because it invokes a certain uncomfortable emotion. Other times a specific concern about a pose or lighting or colors may be legitimate.

If your designer gives you two or three drafts and they all appear equally appealing to you, consider posting them on your blog or Facebook page and asking people to vote. Again, open your mind to options. You do not need to make the decision alone.

It is rare that a draft cover will be exactly what you want the first time. Do not be afraid to ask for changes. However, do it with respect.

Remember, if you really hate the draft design, your upfront communication of expectations might be as much to blame as the designer's interpretation of your description.

Creating your first book cover with a designer is often the most difficult. Once you have established good communications, having a cover designer you trust is an invaluable asset.

Changing designers in the middle of a series will often result in having to redo all previous covers in the series. It is very difficult to copy the exact same aesthetic from one designer to another. Each artist has a look and feel that is most natural to her. For example, some designers tend toward saturated colors while others like soft washes and blurred images. Some designers tend toward more graphic presentations while others prefer realistic imagery blended together.

So, take the time to carefully choose your cover designer. Staying with a designer can ensure that your author brand, series brand, and genre brand are all cohesive and well maintained throughout multiple books.

Chapter Six
BOOK BLURBS AND AUTHOR BIOS

You've completed your manuscript and have exported it for print and ebook. You have a magnificent cover that will draw readers to open the book and read the first chapter. You probably already have a great back cover blurb. Now you are ready to upload your book to a print-on-demand (POD) printer like CreateSpace or Ingram Spark and to all the ebook distributors. You are ready to start selling.

Before you take that final step, however, it is important to look at your book description (blurb) and your author biography in terms of marketing. What you present on vendor sites may be different from what you present in your book. The purpose of distribution sites is to sell, sell, sell. The best way to do that is by making sure your blurbs and bio are short, consistent, and enhance your author brand on every site that features your books. This includes vendor sites, your website, blogs, Facebook, and anywhere else you might be providing that information.

The Book Description That Sells

Most authors are not very good at writing marketing copy. When I write non-fiction I am focused on the details of instruction and the overall structure of how the information is delivered. When I'm finished with the book, the last thing I want to consider is how to write a sales blurb. When I write fiction, I am caught up in a world of my own creation. I am living with characters and places and details that are not real. When I finish a novel it is nearly impossible for me to write good marketing copy.

Tip: Consider writing your marketing copy before you start your book. Even if it's not perfect it will help you to focus the plot and themes. Writing your book blurb first will help you envision the arc of the story and the most important elements to entice a reader. It can help you to start stronger and finish sooner.

Back cover book blurbs follow a tradition based in print publishing. They are written to encapsulate your novel in two to four paragraphs. They are designed for readers browsing a bookstore shelf to quickly ascertain if the story is enough to entice them to open the book and read, then to buy. The blurb paragraphs tend to describe the goals and motivation of the primary character(s); the stakes of the story; and to end with something to entice the reader to open the book. Even if you are not doing print books, ebooks still use the equivalent of a back cover blurb as a long description of the story.

The book blurb you use at distributor sites and in other websites is different from the back cover blurb. First, it is significantly shorter—usually under 150 words. Think of it more like a pitch you would hear on a 15-second commercial for the movie of your book. There is no time for the voice-over actor to read three or four paragraphs. You must capture the tone of the book and the imagination of the reader in four to five sentences.

Most distributor sites today ask for the "short description" and then also provide space for the "long description." Depending on the site, usually the short description is what is displayed with the book. The longer description is reached either through scrolling down the page or clicking on a tab or link.

If the site only allows one description, you should use the short description. This is because when a reader is browsing a book, she will not linger to read four paragraphs. She is evaluating several options and wants to make a decision quickly. If you don't capture that reader in one short paragraph, you may lose her.

I am the first to admit that I am not very good at writing these marketing book blurbs, though I am getting better with practice. I always ask for help. A great resource is finding friends who are scriptwriters or have had scriptwriter training. Their training tends to include a lot of pitches to Hollywood. If you don't know anyone with that background, find an author whose descriptions always pull you in and see if you can get some mentoring.

When I had worked my back cover blurb to only be four paragraphs I was ecstatic. It had started at six. But the idea of getting it down to 100 words was mind-boggling. I turned to writer Jamie Brazil who is also a scriptwriter and enjoys the challenge of this and provided me with some excellent options. Below is an example of how the back cover blurb for my YA Fantasy novel, *Chameleon: The Awakening*, changed to a shorter marketing blurb to use on all vendor sites.

My Beginning Print Back Cover Blurb

No identity. That's what it's like to be a human chameleon, and sixteen-year-old Camryn Painter wonders if she'll ever figure out who the real Camryn is—or should be. Just looking at someone else will cause her body to change into that person. Her parents called it her gift. She calls it her curse.

Then Ohar, a man with impossibly good looks and an ethereal manner offers her a way to claim her birthright by joining the Mazikeen as part of the Forest People. He says she is "the chosen" of the Forest People. The prophecy indicates her powers are beyond any others and she will save their world.

Camryn had always loved the Redwoods at her back door. The stories her mother spun of its inhabitants kept her entertained for much of her childhood. The problem is the stories are real. The forest people are real, human yet not human. They are faery and beasts, evil and angels, mutations of humans and animals over thousands of years. Then there's Dagger, a young man who distrusts the Mazikeen and Ohar, but admits to being a thief and only interested in his own pleasure. All of them want the Chameleon for their own agenda.

With the help of Ohar and Dagger, Camryn learns to control her identity so that she can walk among more than one world. Yet the more Camryn learns, the more she suspects there are too many secrets — dangerous secrets. There are no easy answers, and every decision she makes puts someone's life in danger.

Oy! (picture a slap to my forehead). It's too long even for a back cover. If I had known then what I know now, I would have combined the first two paragraphs and cut the blurb length in half. But it followed all the blurb writing conventions taught by many authors. Below is the revised, much shorter blurb that I now use at all vendor sites, on my website, and whenever I'm writing an article or doing a guest blog.

My Short Marketing Book Blurb

Camryn Painter is a 16-year-old freak of nature. Or possibly the savior of a civilization that isn't supposed to exist. She's a human chameleon... one who transforms into the image of whoever she sees.

Escaping from a medical research facility, Camryn discovers a magical forest world. Not that she's welcome. Her new home is filled with faeries and beasts set on destroying her.

Striking a tribal alliance between what she once believed were mythical beings is her only chance of survival... if she can just control her power and figure out who to trust.

Notice how the marketing blurb still captures the tone of the story— young adult and a little dark. It also captures the cross-genre inclusion of both fantasy and paranormal elements. Though it doesn't discuss the protagonist's specific goals and motivations or any backstory, it clearly suggests the stakes—her survival.

In the *Secrets of Author Marketing* book, we talk a lot about taglines and the importance of a 70-character abstract of the book. Think of the abstract as the movie poster tag line. The marketing blurb expands on that tag line. Strive to keep your marketing blurb under 150 words. To add emphasis, consider combining the tag line as a lead-in to the 100-word blurb. On the Amazon page my description looks like the one below. The combination of the tag line and the marketing blurb gives it the most impact.

Her gifts can save or destroy everyone and everything she loves.

Camryn Painter is a 16-year-old freak of nature. Or possibly the savior of a civilization that isn't supposed to exist. She's a human chameleon… one who transforms into the image of whoever she sees.

Escaping from a medical research facility, Camryn discovers a magical forest world. Not that she's welcome. Her new home is filled with faeries and beasts set on destroying her.

Striking a tribal alliance between what she once believed were mythical beings is her only chance of survival… if she can just control her power and figure out who to trust.

The above, combined with the tagline is only 105 words. Not bad and likely to fit on one book page. Even if it is compressed with a "read more" link (some vendors only give you five lines before a scroll or read more), the most important part is up front—the tagline and the first paragraph.

Need more help in writing blurbs? Here are three blog articles that provide practical help and examples. The first one is from bestselling, thriller author and writing teacher Mike Wellsindie. He has a five-part blurb building method. Be sure to take his fun quiz for distilling longer blurbs into two sentences for practice. http://ht.ly/bNzmd

The next blog post is from bestselling historical Scottish romance author Marti Talbott. The first book in her Highlander series has sold over 50,000 copies.

http://maritalbottstories.blogspot.com/2013/05/how-to-write-book-blurb-that-sells.html

The final article I'd recommend is from writing workshop instructor Marilyn Byerly. What I like about this article is that she gives examples from different genres and explains what needs to change in the blurbs to meet reader expectations in each genre.

http://marilynnbyerly.com/blurb.html

If you can't picture yourself cutting your book blurb down this far, or you really struggle with being objective about what is important to include, then let me reiterate there are people who specialize in this that you can pay a VERY reasonable price to do it for you.

The Blurb Queen, Cathryn Cade

The Literary Midwife, Mary Rosenblum

Both of these women are multi-published authors. They have the knack for taking a two page synopsis and boiling it down to two or three marketing worthy, short paragraphs.

The Author Bio

Just as there is a difference between the back cover blurb and the marketing blurb used to sell the book, the author bio you use at the back of your novel may be different from the author bio you present on vendor pages or attached to articles and guest posts.

Depending on the genre of your book, your author bio at the back of the book might be more personal or friendly. For example, the tradition in romance is to present the author as someone who could be a friend—someone the reader can identify with. Because romance explores some of the most intimate topics in readers' lives, it makes sense that the author bio is written in this tone. Science Fiction, however, has a different tradition. SF readers value an author who has a science background. Highlighting a job in a scientific research facility or at NASA gives the author great credentials in the eyes of readers. Science fiction readers don't necessarily care about the family background or other more personal details because the books are not written to capitalize on that identification in the reader.

Whatever your genre or the style of your current author bio, the key to writing one for marketing purposes is to depict those parts of your biography that indicate you are the best expert to write this book—that your unique background and knowledge gives you inside information. This is particularly critical for non-fiction. And it is an important selling point for fiction.

If you write in multiple genres, you might fashion an author bio for each one. On the other hand, if you deal with similar themes in all your books, one bio might be sufficient. Let me share some examples from my own background and how they have changed over the years.

I write in multiple genres and my books often cross genres. My adult novels have elements of contemporary romance, women's fiction, suspense, science fiction, and paranormal. My current young adult novels are in the juncture between contemporary fantasy and paranormal. I also have a non-fiction book publication career going back to 1998.

Given these disparate genres, until recently I have maintained three separate websites, three distinct author personas, and three different biographies—one for adult fiction, one for young adult fiction, and one for non-fiction. My biographies on each site were far too long. I've provided a shortened version of each one below.

My Adult Fiction Bio

My educational background is in psychology, counseling, computer science, and education. Yes, I have far too many degrees. I just couldn't make up my mind what I wanted to be when I grew up. Somehow I found a way to satisfy both my left and right brain and fashioned a career that could do that by choosing positions that would use my people skills, my love of adaptive technologies, and my desire to be a teacher and mentor.

I am fortunate to now spend the majority of my time journeying into the world of my imagination and writing novels that reflect my passions and my belief that strong women can do anything, that the good guys win in the end, and that love will conquer all.

My Young Adult Fiction Bio

I am the oldest of nine children. This means I can always raise an army to fight off evildoers whenever they appear. It also means I'm a control freak and like to be the boss. Throughout my many career choices, the one constant was writing. The other was never letting reality intrude too far on my fantasy life.

I've finally found the perfect profession. One where I have complete control of entire worlds and the people in them. One where fantasy and reality do more than coexist, they embrace each other. One where I can still induce people to listen to me, to pay attention, and to give me money. Really, what's more fun than that?

My Non-Fiction Bio

Dr. Maggie McVay Lynch is an acclaimed technology teacher and academic computing executive who spent over 30 years in education and computing. After initial careers in corporate technology training, she spent eight years in executive management with two major software companies.

Later in life she completed a doctorate degree in education, allowing her to transfer her technology and teaching skills to academia where she served in positions from Professor to Dean and eventually Chief Information Officer. Maggie ended her career by consulting for both large and small universities, working with teachers and executives to identify appropriate technology for their needs.

Dr. Lynch has previously authored four textbooks by major publishers in London and New York. Also a fiction writer, she has now turned her efforts to helping other authors learn to use technology effectively in their writing business.

Certainly, for the back of a completed book, each of these biographies serves a purpose and meets reader expectations in the genre. The voice for the young adult fiction bio is designed to appeal to both teens and adult readers who like young adult books. It is written as a little more fun. The adult fiction bio attempts to provide enough information to please readers at both ends of the spectrum—those who want a more personalized approach and those who are more interested in specific subject knowledge. Because my books tend to be dark or issue driven, it is written more as a reflection and philosophical approach. The non-fiction bio is exclusively subject knowledge based and designed specifically to market my academic and business expertise for writing educational books.

Of these three, only the non-fiction bio meets the marketing test. My background in teaching and technology matches my non-fiction publications. However, the fiction bios are too "friendly" from a marketing perspective. They do not capitalize on subject matter expertise and they do not offer an incentive for the reader who doesn't know me to take a chance because they don't speak to my qualifications as a career writer.

If I were a USA Today bestselling author, that would be a great marketing lead. It speaks to popularity. If I had won a literary prize, it would speak to quality even if I weren't popular. If I had won a genre book award—the RITA, The Edgar, the Hugo—I would have something to tout. Alas, like the vast majority of authors I can't claim any of these. Without bestseller standing or a major award, for the vast majority of authors the question becomes: "What can I say about myself that convinces a reader to try me?"

The key to the author bio is to sound interesting. When I first began writing novels, I thought I would never find anything interesting to say about myself. I didn't want to talk about my education because I felt it had nothing to do with what I was writing—particularly the romance novels. I definitely didn't want to talk about my family life. No one cares if I am an only child or the oldest of a brood to challenge the Brady Bunch. And I don't write about big families in my books.

When I discussed my dilemma with multi-published and bestselling author Dean Wesley Smith, he said: *"Everyone has something interesting to share. Whether you are a stay-at-home mother who writes in between diaper changes or a librarian who catalogs books, there is something interesting in your life that relates to what you write. All writers include parts of their life in their books. It's all in how you say it."*

Dean found my educational background interesting. Where I saw it as appearing that I couldn't make up my mind about a career, he saw it from a marketing perspective that I was well rounded and can write on almost any subject. He loved that I came from a big family. After all, what better way to understand how to negotiate politics and the psychology of communication? It's like having my own little town. The bottom line is that what I found boring, uninteresting, or just down right bragging, might be exactly what a reader would find fascinating. It is all in how you say it.

When evaluating your own background, consider some of these things and how you can tie them into the books you write.

1. ***Hobbies*** – Do you run marathons? That shows persistence and the ability to overcome adversity. How about flower arranging? Watching movies from the 1940's?
2. ***Work History*** – Even working at McDonald's can provide a plethora of experiences to tie into your subject matter, both humorous and serious. My first job was with Carl's Jr. –a fast food restaurant. After three years I had plenty of stories that became parts of science fiction shorts. Work for a small town newspaper? What incidents did you cover that might relate to your book? Be creative.
3. ***Where You Live*** – Your hometown or current location can be a good marketing focus. If you live in a rural area, and your books take place in the country, capitalize on that. The same goes for urban living. If you've moved around a lot there may be something to tie in there—a story about coming home or finding home perhaps.
4. ***Travel*** – Have you traveled to exotic places that relate to your book? Exotic is in the eye of the beholder. Perhaps your romance takes place in Hawaii and that was where you took your honeymoon. There is a tie-in to romance there. Perhaps your paranormal world or SF planet is filled with

geysers. Tie that to your trip to Yellowstone National Park or to Iceland.
5. **Series** – If you are writing books in a series, once the first book is out you can tag yourself as "the writer of the X series" in your bio. Even better, describe the series with a modifier. "The author of the popular Dark Fae series which challenges the rules of right and wrong."
6. **Pull Quotes** – Reviews, particularly from well-known reviewers or magazines in your genre, can be used in your bio. *"Next Magazine said Maggie Jaimeson's Sweetwater Canyon series is like vinegar and oil, the perfect combination of tart, painful situations wrapped in soothing romantic relationships that leave the reader wanting the next book."*

Always write your marketing bio in third person. Pretend you are the publicist for an up-and-coming new talent. What would you write about you? Use active words throughout. As much as possible match the writing to the voice in your books. If you write humorous books, your bio should have a humorous tone. Dark books or issue books are echoed in a more formal or reflective bio. Ask several people to look it over. Most important, update it when something major happens. Your book has now sold over 100,000 copies? Include that in your bio. If not one book, but all your books together have reached that mark, word your bio to reflect that. Released another book? Update the number of novels you mention in your bio.

What if you've decided to have one bio for all the genres? That does make it difficult, but it might be wise. Due to changes in the publishing landscape and marketing realities, the old idea of having a different pseudonym for each genre has changed. Now authors are advised to encourage as many crossover readers as they can. In that case, you want one website with all your books and one bio that reflects all that you write. In other words, you want a supersite.

Three years ago I faced this dilemma myself. I decided to combine three websites into one in order to capitalize on any cross-promotion for those readers who may move between genres. Those who prefer to only know me in one genre can still find me under the pseudonym that relates to that genre So what did I decide to take from each bio? Below is my combined bio.

Not that the example below is the perfect biography, but it demonstrates how I brought the three personas together into one marketing author bio.

Long Combined Author Bio

With degrees in psychology, counseling, computer science, and education, Maggie Lynch never missed a chance to learn something new. After early careers as diverse as family and marriage counseling and software development, she found a way to satisfy both her left and right brain and fashioned a career in academia that included teaching, faculty leadership, and eventually university executive leadership. Her desire to share her understanding of educational technology has afforded her opportunities to travel around the world, including Europe, Australia, and the Middle East.

Science fiction was Maggie's first love. She sold a number of short stories to SF fiction magazines and tabloids in the mid 1980's and early 1990's. Her focus changed to non-fiction when she joined academia, where she published four textbooks with major NY and London publishers between 1998 and 2007. In 2005, Maggie returned to fiction and her first novel was released in 2011, a romantic suspense. She now writes romance and science fiction under the name Maggie Jaimeson, and young adult fantasy under the name Maggie Faire.

Fortunate to now spend the majority of her time journeying into the world of her imagination, Maggie is happy to be writing novels that reflect her passions. Her novels and her non-fiction reflect her belief that strong women can do anything, that the good guys win in the end, and that love and helping others will conquer all.

Short Combined Author Bio

Maggie Lynch has never missed a chance to learn something new.

With degrees in psychology, counseling, computer science, and education she has had opportunities that have taken her around the world, including Europe, Australia, and the Middle East. Her current publishing credits include nine non-fiction books, a number of science fiction short stories, and nine novels. Now able to spend full time journeying into her imagination, Maggie writes romance and science fiction under the name Maggie Jaimeson, and young adult fantasy under the name Maggie Faire.

Just as with the book blurb, the shorter, marketing bio should be under 100 words. In this instance I focused on the things I hope readers will find most interesting in both non-fiction and fiction of different genres. I focused on my education, my travel, and my publishing credits. Although I can't say I've made a bestseller list or won any major awards, I believe the bio is sufficient to let a reader or media reviewer know that I am a serious, career-oriented writer.

Whether you are releasing your first book or your twentieth make your bio interesting. The nice thing about the short bio is that it leaves room for you to add a line to customize it for particular events. For example, if I'm going to be reading from my YA Fantasy series, I might change the last line to read: *"...and her popular young adult fantasy series, about a human chameleon and the forest people, under the name Maggie Faire."* If I were signing a book in my romance series, I would change the line to reflect that. Because my short bio is only 85 words, I've left room to add enhancements to fit the particular marketing need.

Finally...Remember Nothing is Set in Stone

Though it is wonderful to have these bios ready to go and in all the right places, remember you CAN change them.

As my career has changed and I expand the books I write, I often find a new and temporarily better way to reflect that in my bios. Also as technology changes, the bio length is impacted in the same way the book blurb has been impacted. That is the most important things need to be within the first 50 words or so. Technology also changes the way reader's view and choose books.

Being an author in today's publishing world means adapting, staying agile. Whatever you read here or learn somewhere else is likely to change in the future. It may not change a lot, but it will change enough that small tweaks to book blurbs and bios are worthwhile.

Chapter Seven

THE TRUTH ABOUT ISBNS

All print books sold through bookstores and online require an ISBN. Though most U.S. based online retailers do not require ISBNs to distribute ebooks, there are still some good reasons to have one. In this chapter I will discuss the purpose of the ISBN, the reasons you should obtain ISBNs for both print and ebooks, as well as the costs and trade-offs for where you purchase them and how you use them.

The International Standard Book Number (ISBN) is a unique identifier used around the world to identify, purchase, and sell books. ISBNs first appeared in 1965 as a nine-digit number. Since January 1, 2007, ISBNs have contained 13 digits. A different ISBN is assigned to each edition and variation of a book. A paperback, hardcover, ebook, and audiobook edition would each have its own ISBN. A second edition of a book requires a new ISBN. Reprinting the same book does not require a new ISBN.

Myth: Every ebook type needs a different ISBN. One for EPUB, one for MOBI, and one for PDF.

The above is NOT TRUE! ISBNs relate to the TYPE of book product. Book products currently encompass print, ebook, and audiobook. So, that is three ISBNs total. The one ebook ISBN can be used for EPUB, MOBI, and PDF.

What about multiple languages? You do need a separate ISBN for each language translation. A book in Spanish, although the same story as your English version is still a different book. You need a new ISBN for it. If you choose to use an ISBN for an ebook, you can use the same one for EPUB, MOBI, and PDF in each language.

The graphic below, downloaded from Wikipedia, provides a nice explanation of what each of the digits in an ISBN identifies. It also includes the barcode, which adds the EAN information (Electronic A Number). Bookstores rely on the ISBN for ordering, stocking, and point-of-sale. A number of online retailers of ebooks also rely on this number—particularly Sony and Apple.

To get more specific information go to:
http://en.wikipedia.org/wiki/International_Standard_Book_Number

You do not need a different ISBN for every country. The country is encoded in the "group" digits. You *do* need a different ISBN for each language in which the book is distributed. If the book was published previously by a different publisher, and you have the rights back to the book, you will need a new ISBN. The book is then published as a second edition.

In the digital age of book creation, some authors become concerned that they must have a new ISBN every time they make a change to the book. This is not the case. If you are correcting typos, adding one or two sentences on a page that went astray, or changing the book cover, you do not need a new ISBN. It can still be sold as the same edition. However, making substantial changes such as adding chapters, adding new characters, changing the arc or theme of the story requires a new edition of the book. That edition must have a new ISBN.

In the United States, ISBNs are managed by Bowker, a private for-profit company. You can purchase one ISBN or thousands of ISBNs online at http://myidentifiers.com/ The cost per ISBN decreases if you buy multiple ISBNs at one time.

In some countries, like Canada, there is no cost to get an ISBN because the country wishes to encourage local authors and the government funds the service for managing ISBNs. In those countries, ISBN assignment and management is often run through the Ministry of Culture or through the library system. Other countries are similar to the United States (e.g., the United Kingdom, Ireland, and Australia) and have appointed a private company to do this work. Check with your country's ISBN management authority to determine what costs and paperwork are required to obtain an ISBN. IF you don't know which agency or company manages ISBNs in your country, you can get that information at the non-profit International ISBN organization: http://www.isbn-international.org/agency

Free ISBNs Pros and Cons

Most everyone would prefer not to pay for an ISBN. It is particularly tempting to get a free ISBN when you have no idea if your book will ever make back the costs. There are options to get free ISBNs, even in countries that have a paid service. However, there are tradeoffs when you do that.

First, let's look at why you should make the investment in purchasing your own ISBNs if your country does not offer them for free. There are three important reasons to purchase your own ISBN.

1. You are the publisher of record. Your name or your company name is what is listed on all sites and bibliographic reference feeds.
2. You want full control of the ISBN and the content provided to all bibliographic feeds.
3. If you decide you want to have your book printed elsewhere (e.g., move POD printing from CreateSpace to Ingram Spark or to a mass market printing company) you can move it without getting a new ISBN. It's your ISBN as a publisher.

What is the cost? If you are purchasing from Bowker, buying a single ISBN is outrageously priced at $125.00. Therefore, it is wise to purchase at least a group of 10 ISBNs at $250.00, which brings the price down to $25.00 per ISBN. Ten ISBNs represents five books in both print and ebook format. With a plan to write five books during your career, it is worth buying that block of ten. ISBNs do not have an expiration date.

What if you are only writing one book or you can't afford the $250.00 to purchase ten ISBNs? There are alternatives to purchasing from Bowker. You can acquire a free ISBN from a POD publisher like CreateSpace. Or you can pay $10 and be able to list yourself or your publishing company as the publisher. In both those cases, if you ever decide to publish a print book without CreateSpace you will need to purchase your own ISBN. CreateSpace also offers a $99 version to purchase that would allow you to take the ISBN with you.

Other POD printers offer ISBNs ranging from $2.00 to $10.00 each. Like CreateSpace, these low cost ISBNs are owned by the publisher and cannot be moved. So, if you decide not to publish there anymore you will need to purchase your own.

Many authors go ahead with the free or $10 ISBN to cut costs. If your book takes off and you want to establish your own ISBNs you can still later change your mind, purchase your own ISBN, and put up a second edition of the book.

Aggregators are companies that provide services to authors and then directly interface with retailers. Before the ebook revolution, those services were companies like Lulu and Xlibris. Now there are many companies specifically designed to help authors interface with markets for both print and ebooks. Smashwords, Draft 2 Digital, StreetLib, Vearsa, Book Baby, Fast Pencil, and Xin Xii are examples of ebook aggregators.

Some author service companies require you to use their ISBN in order to take advantage of the services. Other companies allow you to use your own. Still others, like CreateSpace, allow you to use your own ISBN but it limits your distribution options. For example, at Create-

Space if you use their ISBN you get library distribution. If you use your own, you don't.

The most important disadvantage to using an ISBN from an aggregator is the coding of the publisher identification digits. ISBNs have a prefix that is permanently associated with the publisher who purchased the ISBNs from Bowker.

For example, when CreateSpace purchases a block of a hundred thousand ISBNs from Bowker, the company then assigns those ISBNs to authors who wish to have a free ISBN. As Bowker is the official manager of ISBNs in the United States, it assigns all numbers in this block to reflect CreateSpace as the publisher. When you accept an ISBN from CreateSpace, it means that CreateSpace is listed as the publisher on all systems around the world and in all bookstores.

Is this a problem? Rumor has it that some bookstores have a policy of not dealing with Amazon. CreateSpace is an Amazon subsidiary company and therefore they will not order books from them. For other bookstores it is not a problem. Personally, I don't think it is as a big a deal as some people do. Only the most anti-Amazon stores are going to be looking at the ISBN number of every book they order, noticing the publisher identifier is Amazon and then refusing to order it. I can't imagine that happening on any regular basis.

One other way to obtain an ISBN at less cost is to join a publishing cooperative. This is a group of authors who join together and agree to publish under the same publisher name. Windtree Press and Book View Café are two examples of this. Cooperatives are different from a commercial publisher in that titles are not purchased or contracted; and the cooperative does not employ full-time editors, cover designers, and formatters. A publishing cooperative allows a group of independent authors to share costs and resources in their publishing efforts.

For example, at Windtree Press the cooperative purchases a block of ISBNs to be shared among all the members. Each member then pays a pro-rated cost for the ISBN. Purchasing a block of 100 ISBNs reduces the cost for each ISBN to $5.75. A larger cooperative with 100 members may be able to purchase a block of 1,000 ISBNs. In theory, the cooperative could choose to then make each ISBN available to members at a reimbursement cost of only $1.00. In larger cooperatives it is common for them to mark up the actual ISBN cost in order to pay someone to enter the book information in Bowker's database. But even at $5.00 per ISBN, members realize a great savings.

Members of co-ops still face some of the same disadvantages as they do to purchasing ISBNs from an aggregator like CreateSpace. The publisher of record is the co-op press name (i.e., Windtree Press or Book View Café). Depending on the bylaws of the co-op, if a member leaves the co-op she may need to purchase another ISBN and redistribute books as a second edition. Even if the co-op allows the ISBN to transfer with the member, as Windtree Press does, it is likely she will still want a different publisher identified for all her books.

Ebook ISBNs

First you are NOT required to have ebook ISBNs. Every major vendor (Amazon, Kobo, Apple, B&N, Google) either uses its own stock identifier (e.g., ASIN for Amazon) or puts in a "dummy" ISBN number if you don't supply one. If the vendor deals with partners in places around the world that require an ISBN, they generate it as needed.

So, why would you even bother with an ebook ISBN? Most tracking organizations for bestseller lists (NYT, USA Today, Wall Street Journal, etc.) track books by ISBN. All of these also have ebook bestseller lists. Without an ISBN for your ebook, your book will not be tracked for those lists and thus not reported to booksellers and libraries, in newspapers and magazines, or to other media.

In addition, all third party databases find and report on books by ISBN. Bowker itself provides free listing of books (print and ebook based on ISBN) in various directories such as Books in Print, which is used by schools, libraries, and bookstores to decide which books to purchase.

For me, I choose to have an ebook ISBN because I want to improve the metadata that's available to all sites around the world where my book is distributed. However, I have lessened my personal costs by being part of an author cooperative that can purchase ISBNs 100 at a time and have the cost to me be only $5.75.

Is it required? No. Is it useful? In my opinion, absolutely.

How to Use Bowker Effectively

If you have decided to purchase your own ISBNs and you live in the United States, you will need to use the services at Bowker. You do all of this online via the site at http://myidentifiers.com

The first step is purchasing the ISBNs. You can buy a block of ISBNs without having to provide any information except you as a publisher and your credit card information. Once you access the myidentifiers.com site, click on **Buy ISBNs** in the menu.

A screen appears with several options ranging from the purchase of a single ISBN for $125 to pricing on blocks of ISBNs at 10, 100, and 1,000. Click on the item that represents the number of ISBNs you wish to purchase. Once selected, you will be taken directly to the shopping cart screen.

Tip: If you are purchasing more than one ISBN be sure that the number entered in the shopping cart represents the bulk group. In the example below, the author elected to purchase the 10 ISBN package. In the shopping cart it shows the number one. That is correct. The author is purchasing only one package. Do **not** put the number 10 in this section.

Click on the **Checkout** button to complete your purchase.

On the checkout page you will see a number of other offers. I advise you *not* to select any of these. Bar codes can be generated for free at http://bookcovers.creativindie.com/free-online-isbn-barcode-generator/ Also, if you are using CreateSpace or Ingram Spark as your print book distributor, they will put the barcode on your backcover automatically if you don't have one. Widgets and Apps can be developed in other venues for significantly less money. The best course of action is to purchase the ISBNs at Bowker and nothing else.

Like all ecommerce engines on the Internet, the checkout process will require you to create an account, choose a password, provide your credit card information, billing address, and phone.

After the payment is processed, the ISBNs are immediately added to your account. To view them go to the **My Account** menu option and select **Manage ISBNs**.

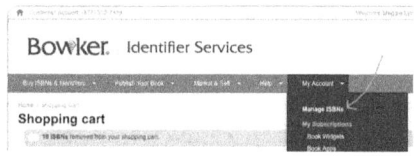

Once those ISBNs are displayed in your account, you can assign current and future titles to them. At any time between the purchase and the release of your book, you can go in and fill in the required fields to make sure your book information is associated with a specific ISBN number. Most authors choose to do this very close to their book release date, or just after release, because that is when they have all of the information for the book. You may go back and change things at any time until you click **Submit**.

Once you hit SUBMIT you can no longer change the title, the publication date, or the book type (e.g., print or ebook). However, you may change other elements like the description, page count, categories, etc.

Another thing Bowker offers is for you to upload a PDF version of the book. They use this to create more metadata about the books, capturing hundreds of more keywords. They do not sell or distribute the PDF version anywhere. This is not required, but I do recommend it.

When you first go to **Manage ISBNs** in your account, a screen with each ISBN you purchased is presented and a button to Assign Title.

If you have purchased a block of ISBNs and already know titles for books, you may wish to enter them all at this time. However, that is not required. You may return to this screen at any time in the future and enter the information, as the book is ready for publication.

Tip: Enter the information for your print book and ebook in the same sitting. This will be more efficient allowing you to clone information and then make changes that apply to that format.

Bowker provides numerous opportunities for you to enter metadata that will be transferred via their *Books in Print* publication and feeds to booksellers and libraries. However, only a few of those fields are required. It is up to you how much information you wish to provide. Remember, the more information you provide, the easier it is for booksellers and librarians to find your titles in a search. All *required* field entries are marked with a small red asterisk.

Begin the entry process by clicking on the **Assign Title** button in the **Manage ISBNs** section of your account. This will take you to the first screen in the data entry process. Notice that next to each field is a question mark button. This is context sensitive help relating to that item.

The first screen in the data entry process is the **Title Details** screen. The only required field on this first screen is the **Title**. However, there are several other fields I recommend you take the time to enter.

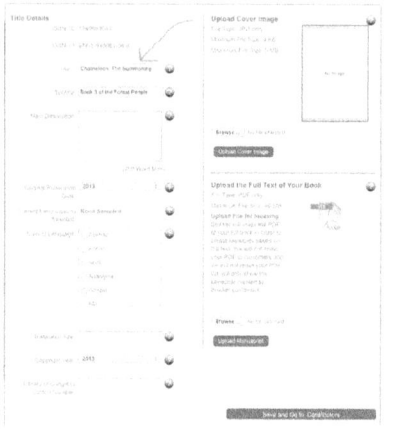

For non-fiction books with a subtitle, be sure to enter the subtitle exactly as it appears on the book cover. For example, the title of this book is *Secrets Every Author Should Know*. The subtitle is *Indie Publishing Basics*. In this instance the primary title is entered in the **Title** field. The subtitle is entered in the **Subtitle** field exactly as it appears on the book cover. If the subtitle on your book cover contains initial caps, then that is the way it should be entered in the **Subtitle** field in Bowker.

Fiction titles work the same way, though few fiction titles also have a subtitle. If the fiction title is part of a series, I have a work-around suggestion. Enter the series name in the **Subtitle** field. This is because the data entry screens provide no place to enter a series title. If your book has a subtitle and is also part of a series, you have a choice to make. You may include the subtitle in the title line as I did in the example, or you may decide to put it in the **Subtitle** field.

In my YA fantasy series, each of the seven books has the name "Chameleon" as the first part of the title. This maintains continuity between books and references the primary character. This is similar to how the Harry Potter books were presented. My subtitle then refers to the next step in the series: *Chameleon: The Awakening* and *Chameleon: The Choosing* for example. The series title is *The Forest People*. To include all of the information that is on the cover, I put the title and subtitle in the **Title** field. Then I put the series title in the **Subtitle** field with the book number: *Book 1 of The Forest People*.

Tip: When including the subtitle with the title, do not use a colon as the separator. Though Bowker accepts a colon in the title field without incident. CreateSpace does not. The CreateSpace software reads a colon in the title as a subtitle. This then causes an error when CreateSpace tries to match the ISBN with the Bowker record. Therefore, in both the Bowker record and the CreateSpace record use a hyphen, **Chameleon – The Awakening**, instead of a colon.

The **Main Description** field is where you will enter the short blurb (100 words) you worked on in the previous chapter. Although Bowker allows you to have a description of up to 350 words, it is best to use the marketing description here just as you will in all other places on the web. In that way, it will match wherever a reader or bookseller encounters your title. You will have an opportunity to provide a longer description on many vendor sites.

The **Original Publication Date** is for this particular edition and format of the book. If you are planning your books in advance, use the drop down arrow to select the year in which you anticipate publishing this work.

In the **Current Language** box, scroll down to select the check box next to **English**. Be careful *not* to select **Middle English**, which is right under the word English. If you are uploading a book in another language, select it here.

The **Copyright Year** should match the original publication year. Again, just like the publication year, the copyright is the year this particular work in this particular format existed as a whole unit.

The **Library of Congress Control Number** (LCCN) can be entered after you release the book. Because you are required to send a copy of the book when you register the copyright, most authors do not complete this entry until after the book is released and a LCCN has been sent to them. (See the next chapter on Copyright Registration for this process).

On this same data entry page, you may also upload your book cover. This is highly recommended. Notice the file size limitations. I suggest uploading the same book cover size that will be used for all vendor sites. That is typically about 2100 pixels on the long side. Those files tend to be well under 5 MB. To complete the upload, click on the **Browse** button to find the book cover file in your computer. Then click on the **Upload Cover Image** button to complete the upload.

The final option on this first data entry page is to upload a **PDF** file of your completed manuscript. This allows Bowker to scan the entire manuscript and generate search terms. There is no place within the Bowker system to do keywords or other description types as are allowed on most retailer sites. Scanning the PDF file is the way in which Bowker indexes keywords for the manuscript.

Bowker does not make a copy of your manuscript available to anyone. The company does not offer your manuscript for sale. It is simply used to create an index of subject headings and keywords for search. Again, I highly recommend uploading your completed manuscript. To complete the upload first click on the **Browse** button to locate the manuscript file in your computer. Then click on the **Upload Manuscript** button to complete the process.

When you have completed all the fields you wish to complete on this screen, click on the **Save and Go To: Contributors** button. Don't worry if you didn't have all of the information to enter. Remember, the only thing you cannot change once you submit is the title and publication date.

The contributor screen is used primarily to enter the author information. The only required field on this screen is to enter one contributor. If there are multiple authors, you have the option to enter each one. If your book has other contributors you wish to include, such as an illustrator for a children's book, this is also the section in which you would add that person under the **Add More Contributors** button.

Begin the process by entering your author name in the designated fields marked **First** and **Last**. If you are using a pen name that is what is entered here.

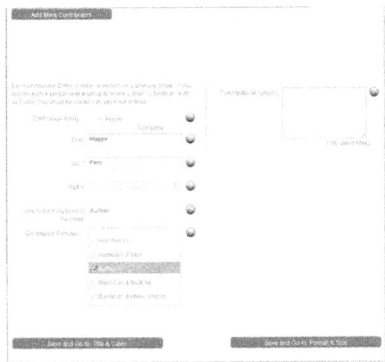

By default the **Person** option is selected as the **Contributor Entity**. If a company instead of an individual authored your book, then click on the button above **Company**. This is rare for novelists, but not uncommon for non-fiction work. It is possible, for example, that an organization focused on health issues might author several books on health as a company.

In the **Contributor Function** box, scroll down to select **Author** by clicking in the check box to the left of the entry.

If there are multiple author contributors to the work, as in an anthology, you have the opportunity to enter each one by clicking on the **Add More Contributors** button above the first and last name. Be aware that the order of contributors is important in this instance.

The first contributor entered is guaranteed to be displayed in the *Books In Print* publication and feed.

Though not required, it is recommended that you complete the **Contributor Biography** field. This is where you would enter the short bio (under 100 words) you completed in the previous chapter. Remember, the *Books In Print* product is sent to libraries and booksellers. It is what they use to determine which books to purchase. From the *Books in Print* listing, the library or bookseller has several options to purchase the book from their vendor of choice (e.g., Ingram, Baker & Taylor, Overdrive, etc.)

The third data entry screen describes the book type. This is where the medium and format of the book are detailed, as well as the subjects that suggest how to categorize the book.

The required fields are Medium, **Format**, and **Primary Subject**. Each is selected by clicking on the up or down arrow in the right side of the entry field.

Medium describes what type of a book it is: print, ebook, or audiobook. Let's look at entering a print book first.

If the ISBN relates to your print book, select the **Print** option under the **Medium** field. Next, move to the format field. The choices are **Hardback** or **Paperback**. Most self-published authors will select

Paperback. Finally, scroll through the **Format Details** box to select **Trade paperback (US).** If you are in the UK or a country that uses UK sizing, select **Trade Paperback (UK).**

Most authors do not fill in the height, width, and weight of the book. This is used to calculate shipping costs when libraries or booksellers order the book. However, it is not critical for you to enter, as most libraries and booksellers order print books from Ingram or Baker & Taylor. Your POD printer (e.g., CreateSpace, Lightning Source, Ingram Spark) will send the actual final dimensions and weight to distributors like Ingram and Baker & Taylor if you have selected that option.

If the ISBN relates to your ebook, select **Ebook** in the **Medium** field. In the **Format** field there will only be one option to select; **Electronic Book Text.** There are no options for size with an ebook.

The next important field is **Primary Subject.** This is your opportunity to define the subject for your book. Bowker subjects are a proprietary schema used within the *Bowker Books In Print* product. It uses the same phrasing and structure as the Library of Congress Subject Headings (LCSH). There are over 80,000 subject possibilities available. However, the drop down options present only the highest level descriptors.

Authors may find this restricting. However, these selections are only temporary until the book is indexed (another reason to provide that PDF copy). Then catalogers will create the permanent subject descriptors. In order to have the subject changed, you will need to email Bowker support and request a change.

When you have completed all the options you wish to provide on this screen, click on the **Save and Go To: Sales & Pricing** button at the bottom of the screen.

Sales & Pricing is the final data screen prior to finalizing and submitting your book to be placed on the *Books in Print* list.

Bowker provides options for sales and pricing in six countries: Australia, Canada, New Zealand, Spain, the United Kingdom, and the United States. Enter the sales and pricing information for each country in which you wish the information to be distributed. I recommend entering the information for all six countries. Though you may put all pricing in US dollars, it is much easier for international buyers to calculate costs and budget if it is in their own currency. This screen is also where you must enter the actual publication date and a target audience.

You must enter the required fields of **Where is the Title Sold** (Country), **Publication Date, Audience, Currency, Price**, and **Price Type** for each country. Use the drop down arrows to select a country under the **Where is the Title Sold field**. When a country is selected the appropriate flag appears in the top bar. This allows you to make changes to fields depending on the country selected. For example, a publisher might choose to release a book in the United States in one month and in other countries two or three months later. Personally, I prefer that the book be released in all countries at once. Most authors uploading to distributors select all possible venues at the same time. Once you have entered the first country data, all fields will remain the same until you select a new country.

Let's look at the fields that may not be as obvious.

Title Status for most authors will be **Active Record**, which is the default. However, you do have the option of making other selections based on your planning calendar and how you wish to handle availability. Other popular options include forthcoming, inactive, and out of print.

Target Audience is fairly easy for **Young Adult** audience books (ages 12-18). For an audience under age 12 choose **Juvenile Audience**. You can limit that further with the **From Age** and **To Age** fields. Confusion sometimes occurs, however, in the adult audience options. In the illustration below there are four possible options for an adult audience. The only one that works for fiction is **Trade.** The other options are for non-fiction audience designations.

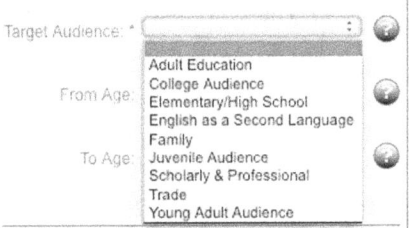

The pricing and currency fields should be carefully evaluated. As I stated earlier, it is best to provide your books in the currency of the country. For this reason you may want to have a currency calculator open in another tab while entering these fields. My favorite one is the one that is at the top of the page in Google when you enter "currency calculator" in the search field. You enter the price in **US Dollar**, and then select the next box drop down arrow for the country you wish to calculate. It immediately provides a price.

Most consumers expect pricing to be at an even dollar amount or in the 95 or 99-cent category. Pricing a book at $4.50 instead of $4.99 looks unusual in comparison to larger publisher pricing. In foreign currency round up or down to reach the even dollar or 95 or 99-cent equivalent.

Tip: Canadian, Australian, and New Zealand dollars all tend to run within fifty cents of the same price in US dollars. Instead of putting in an odd price (e.g., 4.62 Australian dollars), consider simply making the price the same across all of these countries. You may gain or lose a few cents, but the pricing looks more professional.

Once you have completed all the fields on this screen, and you are confident in your all entries, click the **Submit** button to make the record with this ISBN permanent. That means you may not change the title or publication dates. However, if you are not prepared to submit yet, then select the left button: **Save and Go To: Format & Size.** This will save all your entries on the **Sales & Pricing** screen but not yet submit the record for finalization.

I recommend doing the final **Submit** the day before your release on other platforms. In that way, you will be certain of the publication date and the title will certainly have been permanently enshrined on your cover.

Chapter Eight
COPYRIGHT REGISTRATION

Some writers mistakenly believe that getting an ISBN for a book automatically registers the copyright. **It does not!** They are two different processes. ISBNs are obtained in the United States through a private company, Bowker, that manages the database for all books identified by ISBN. The purpose of an ISBN is simply to have a unique identifier for a book so that it can be sold and tracked globally. Think of it as an inventory code that is the same for every retailer around the world.

Copyright registration has nothing to do with sales of your book or making it available to retailers. In fact, you can register a copyright for a book you never plan to sell or make available outside your immediate family. You are not required to have an ISBN to register a copyright.

Copyright registration is managed through the United States Copyright Office, which is part of the Library of Congress. It is the official United States government body that maintains records of copyright registrations. It is used by copyright title searchers who are attempting to clear a chain of title for copyrighted works.

An analogy I like to use when describing copyright registration is the one most people understand for obtaining title for property. If you own a car in the United States, you receive title to that car from your state government. That title is in the form of a certificate that proclaims you are the owner. The title includes a description of your car, including the vehicle identification number (VIN). If you rent the car out or loan the car to someone else, you still own it and can have use of it. However, if you sell the car you must transfer the title to the new owner. Once that happens, you no longer have use of the car and no say in what happens to the car.

If there were no car titles, a thief could steal your car and claim it was his. You would have little recourse to get the car back because you would have no proof that you own the car. The proof of ownership is the title certificate.

Registering your copyright provides a certificate from the federal government recognizing that you own the rights to your book. In principle, your work is protected by copyright the moment it takes form. However, without this certificate of registration it is difficult to prove you are the owner if another person brings a copy of your work forward and claims it is hers.

As with holding title to a car, you have rights associated with your written work. Those rights allow you to "rent" your work to someone else. This is what happens when you sign a contract with a publisher. The publisher is paying for the right to use what you wrote to make a profit. However, you are still the owner of that work. Based on the contract, the publisher can only make money from your work for a certain period of time. There may also be ways in which you can end your relationship so that the publisher can no longer use your work.

You also have the right to "sell" your work to someone else. This usually happens when you do a work-for-hire contract or a ghostwriter contract. In these contracts a publisher or individual is paying you for the work as though you were an employee. Once that payment is complete (e.g., a specific fee or royalties over a specified time period), the buyer owns your work. You no longer have the legal right to sell that work again or use it in any way.

In both of these examples—and in self-publishing—registering your copyright is what helps to establish that you are, in fact, the original owner of the work. If a dispute occurs, you will want that certificate of registration and the date it was filed in order to prove you are the owner. If there are two separate registration certificates issued for the same book, by two different people (yes, it does happen), the earlier registration has a better chance of being successful in a lawsuit than the later one.

At this time I must provide a caveat. The above illustrations demonstrate how not having a certificate of registration may cause problems. However, I am not an attorney. Therefore, do not take anything I say as legal advice. As I discuss copyright law throughout this chapter, I will reference quotations from the United States Copyright Office or a website that provides legal advice.

If you are unclear about your own copyright situation or how copyright registration laws apply to a specific book, seek advice from an intellectual property attorney licensed to practice in the your country or jurisdiction. Do not rely on what you find on the Internet or in books such as mine to provide legal advice. The law is complex and interpretations change as cases are tried in court. It is important to analyze what the latest case law findings say when making a decision on your own situation. Only a licensed attorney can give you that advice.

Registering your copyright with the United States Copyright Office is voluntary. The copyright office summarizes the reasons for registration on their website:

"Copyright exists from the moment the work is created. However, if you wish to bring a lawsuit for infringement of a work sold in the United States you will need to have registered. Registered works may be eligible for statutory damages and attorney's fees in successful litigation. If registration occurs within five years of publication, it is considered prima facie evidence in a court of law."

(See Circular 1, *Copyright Basics*
   at http://www.copyright.gov/circs/circ1.pdf)

In other words, even though your work is protected from the moment of creation, you can't bring a lawsuit to recover lost income or assess damages against someone who steals your work unless it is registered.

In addition, registering within three months of publication is advised. According to NOLO, a publisher of legal information:

"You can register a copyright at any time, but registering it promptly may pay off in the long run. Timely registration—that is, registration within three months of the work's publication date or before any copyright infringement actually begins—makes it much easier to sue and recover money from an infringer. Specifically, timely registration creates a legal presumption that your copyright is valid, and allows you to recover up to $150,000 (and possibly lawyer fees) without having to prove any actual monetary harm."

http://www.nolo.com/legal-encyclopedia/copyright-registration-notice-enforcement-faq-29067.html

The least costly and quickest copyright registration method is through electronic registration at the United States Copyright Office website: https://eco.copyright.gov/ The cost for this is only $35.00 per book, and you may send an electronic copy of the book with your registration. You can pay by credit or debit card, or by electronic funds transfer using check routing and account information. Once the payment is accepted you will immediately receive a tracking number and a temporary registration number. Approximately 90 days later (depending on how many registrations the copyright office is processing) you will receive the official registration certificate in the mail.

An alternate registration method is through the mail. The cost to do a mailed registration is $65.00. You may download the form from the copyright office, and you must pay by check or money order. The office does not accept credit card payments through the mail. With the mailed form you must send **two** printed copies of the book to the copyright office. The processing time for this is significantly longer—often taking up to six months.

Even authors of commercial publishers should check if a copyright has been registered on their behalf. Most small presses, and even some large publishers do not do any copyright registration for their authors unless they are bestsellers. Check your contracts. If your books have not been registered, it is recommended that you register them now.

My personal process is to register my copyright within one week of release. Though I have not yet had a need to file an infringement lawsuit, I want to be sure the registration is as early as possible.

I've heard authors tell me they aren't going to register their work because they don't want to pay the fee, or they don't believe their "little, unknown work" will be stolen, or because they are not in a financial position to hire an attorney and bring a lawsuit if it were stolen. Certainly, registration is voluntary. Personally, I look at it as inexpensive insurance.

I wish we lived in a world where no one plagiarized written work, or outright stole books and put a different author name on it. Unfortunately, it happens far too often, and electronic document transmission has made it even easier for criminals to do this.

In addition, the likelihood of infringement increases with the popularity of a book or an author. You never know when you will become popular. You may work in obscurity for six years and then suddenly a book hits the New York Times list or it wins a major award. Once you become popular, not only is the bestselling book a temptation for criminals, but your entire backlist is targeted as well. Criminals have been known to put a new author name on a book and immediately register the copyright. They will even keep the same title (titles cannot be copyrighted). If you have not registered, what recourse do you have? None.

For me, spending $35.00 and a little time online is a small price to pay for the assurance that I can bring a lawsuit to prove infringement.

Convinced to register? Let's go through the online copyright process.

Go to: https://eco.copyright.gov/ Watch for a notice about pop-ups in the upper part of your screen. Elect to allow pop-ups from the copyright.gov site.

Note: The site works well with Internet Explorer and Firefox

Browsers. It may have problems with other browsers, including Chrome.

You should first see the login screen. This is where you can set up an account with the copyright office by creating your login ID and password.

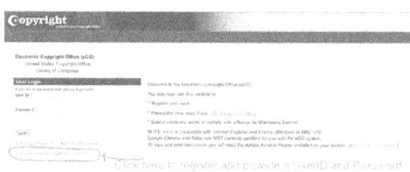

Once you have set up an account, you will see a screen with several menu options. To register your copyright, select the **Register a New Claim** option under the **Copyright Services** heading.

Some authors have become confused with the language of registering a claim, mistakenly thinking this means you are claiming an infringement. This actually indicates you are registering your claim as the legal owner of the copyright.

The next screen determines what type of registration you want. A single work, created by one person, solely owned by one person is the default. This is the case for the majority of self-publishing authors. If the statements are all true, click in the **Yes** box next to each one. Then click the **Start Registration** button at the bottom.

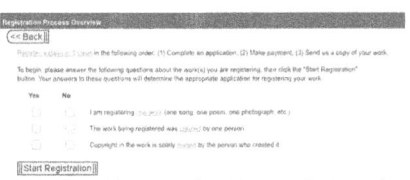

If any of the statements are not true, click in the **No** box and you will be taken to a different form. I will illustrate the process for the default use—a single work, created by one person, solely owned by one person. After checking each Yes box, when you click the **Start Registration** button a window will pop up asking you to confirm your selections.

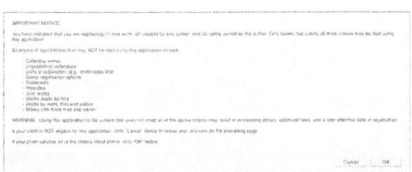

The notice reminds you what you selected and gives examples of the types of registrations that may not be used with the form you will be taken to next. Assuming you still wish to continue, click the **OK** button on the lower right of the screen.

Finally, you will be taken to a screen to start the actual application process. The Copyright Office wishes to be helpful, but unfortunately, the next screen appears confusing. All the links in the center of the screen are to describe the different types of work you may choose and offer extended definitions.

You should go directly to the bottom of the screen and click on the drop down arrow to choose **Literary Work.**

The elements presented on the left will continue to appear on each subsequent screen in the process. This is a tracking system, as well as a menu navigation system. The red arrow on the far left in the navigation tool indicates the screen you have currently selected. In this case it is the **Type of Work** screen.

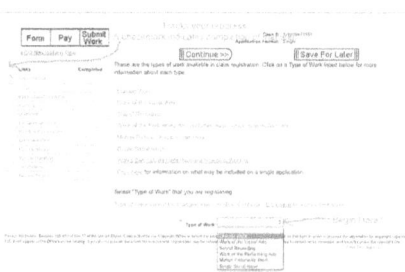

On each screen you have two options presented by the buttons at the top. Option one is to **Continue**. Clicking this will take you to the next screen in the forward navigation. Option two is to **Save For Later**. This allows you to save whatever you have completed thus far and return to it at any time. Now that you have an account, you can log in again and start where you left off.

Once you have selected **Literary Work** click the **Continue** button.

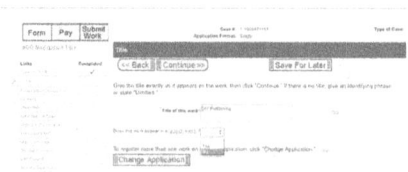

Enter the title of your book exactly as it appears on your title page.

The form only allows your title to be one line long. If you have a subtitle, it doesn't need to be put here. The software will think you are trying to register more than one title. In the above example, I entered **DIY Publishing** and not the subtitle.

The next question asked is: **Does this work appear in a larger work**? If this is a stand-alone book the answer is usually **No**. Click the dropdown arrow to select the answer appropriate for you.

You would answer **Yes** if, for example, this were a short story that was first published in a collection of stories. You would also answer yes is if you had published a novel earlier, then took the first chapter and turned it into a short story. Even though you may have changed a sentence or two, the substantive part of your story was published in the novel previously. Answering **Yes,** generates a screen that requires you to enter information about the copyright and registration of the larger work so that information can be appropriately matched with your copyright registration for the current work.

For example, this book has several chapters that were originally created in my DIY Publishing book. I have updated the content, but much of the content is substantially the same. Therefore, when I registered the copyright for this book I listed DIY Publishing as the first occurrence of some of the content.

Once you have selected the appropriate response, **Yes** or **No**, click the **Continue** button.

The next screen will ask about the publication status of the work you are registering: **Has this work been published?** If I am completing the registration after the book has been released for sale, I select **Yes** on this option. You *are* allowed to register a copyright for a book that has not been released or may never be released for sale. Selecting **Yes** to indicate the book has been published, will pop up a screen asking ask for the publication month, day, and year.

The next screen asks about author information. Only two items are required on this screen (indicated by red asterisks). They are the country in which you hold citizenship or residence, and what contributions the author made to the book. You may select as many boxes as are appropriate to your involvement with the book. I select only the **Text** box because I have someone else who designs the cover and another person who does the editing. Your situation may differ.

Tip: You have a choice whether to use a pen name or not. If your book copyright page uses only your pen name, you will want to type that name in the **Pseudonym** box. If you do not want your real name revealed in public records, do not fill out the name information in the **Individual Author** boxes.

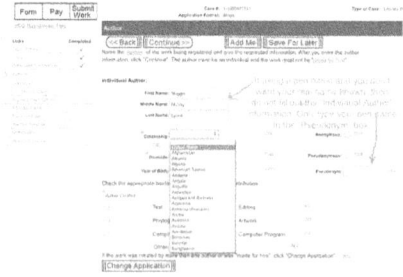

Click the **Continue** button to go to the next screen.

The next screen is where you enter your address. Because you already have a profile related to your account, you can click the **Add Address** button to have the address automatically filled from that information. If you wish to use a different address than what is in your profile, do so here. This information is a public record. Click **Continue** when completed.

The **Limitation of Claim** screen, shown below, is one screen that the majority of self-published authors will not need. It is used only if the work is based on pre-existing work. For example, if your book is an analysis of Grimms' fairy tales and each fairy tale is included in your work, you need to use the limitation screen. This screen allows you to provide the copyright details of the other work(s) and delineate which parts of the book are uniquely yours. It is that unique part that will be registered to you.

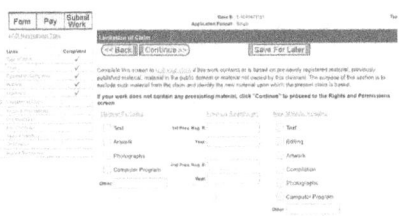

Click **Continue** to skip this limitation screen.

The next screen, **Rights and Permissions,** asks for specific contact information should someone request permission to use your work. If you have a publishing entity (highly recommended) that is separate from your individual identity, you would enter that information under the **Organization** column on the right side of the screen. If you do not have a separate company, then enter your legal name and address under the **Individual** column on the left side of the screen.

Remember, this is the contact information that would be provided to anyone who requests it. So, be careful when selecting what address you wish to provide. Many authors without a publishing entity will only provide a post office box address. Click **Continue** when you have completed the form.

The next screen asks whom the Copyright Office should contact with questions. If your publishing company is large enough to have staff or an answering service, you might choose to put that organization name, address, and phone number here. Otherwise, complete the individual contact side and use your personal or author-specific email address and phone.

The next screen is another that the majority of self-publishing authors will not use. It is the **Special Handling** screen, and carries a fee of $750.00 if it applies to your situation. It is used by those who are already involved in a lawsuit about the rights of this work, have customs issues or have unusual deadline issues. If it doesn't apply to you, simply click the **Continue** button.

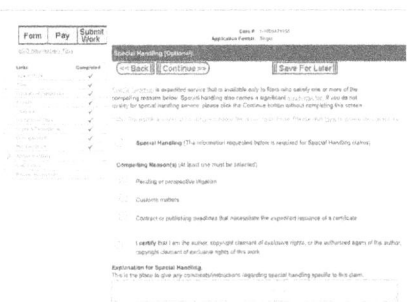

Finally, you have reached the screen where you **certify** that you are indeed the author of this book and that everything you have included on the application is correct. The statement reads:

I **certify** that I am the author, copyright claimant, or owner of exclusive rights, or the authorized agent of the author, copyright claimant, or owner of exclusive rights of this work and that the information given in this application is correct to the best of my knowledge.

Click in the box next to the certification statement. Then type your name in the box labeled **Name of certifying individual**.

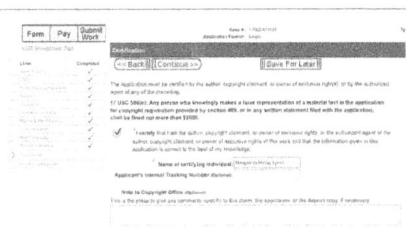

Click **Continue** when you have certified your claim that the copyright should be registered to you.

The final screen before checkout and paying your $35.00 is a review screen. It displays everything you have entered as it appears in the database. Corrections cannot be made on this screen. Click on the appropriate navigation item on the left to return to the screen where you can change the information.

Once you are satisfied with all of your entries, click on the **Add to Cart** button at the top of the page. This will take you to a check out system where you pay the fee to register your copyright.

If you are not ready to do that yet, click on the **Save for Later** button at the top of the page. This will allow you to save everything you've entered and return to it at another time.

The uploading of the electronic copy of your book comes after you have paid the fee. However, before I illustrate that upload process, let's take a look at how to get back to your application should you decide to **Save for Later.**

First, login to the site at https://eco.copyright.gov/

Knowing where to look for your application is not intuitive. On the left navigation bar, under **Check Registration Case Status**, select **Working Cases.**

This will bring up a screen showing any incomplete applications. Click on the link to the application you wish to review and complete.

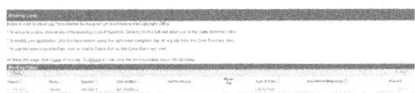

Once you click on the link you will be returned to the familiar screens with the navigation on the left and whichever screen you have selected on the right. Continue to work through the application as described above until you are ready for checkout and payment.

Remember: Once you have checked out, that registration record becomes permanent. You cannot return to make changes.

After the check out and payment is complete, click the **Continue** button to upload a copy of your completed book. A payment receipt with your case number will be sent to the email you provided in the application.

Under the **Electronic Deposit Upload** header, click on the link that reads **Upload Deposit.** This will open the file manager on your computer and allow you to browse and select the appropriate file.

The copyright office accepts many file types for upload:

- Microsoft Word Documents (.doc or .docx)
- Adobe documents (.pdf)
- Web page formats (.htm or .html)
- Rich text format (.rtf)
- Text documents (.txt)
- Word Perfect documents (.wpd)
- Microsoft Works documents (.wps)

I recommend uploading a **PDF file** because it retains both the content and the formatting of your book. As you are likely already creating a PDF file for your print-on-demand printer and for electronic download, it is easiest to send this same file to the Copyright Office as the deposit of your work.

The screenshot below from the U.S. Copyright Office's PowerPoint presentation illustrates the upload process.

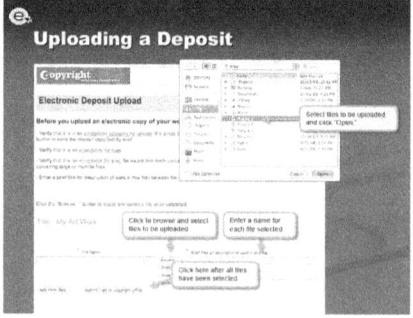

If you completed the form to upload a single work from a single author, then you will only have one file to upload. Note the **Name** field associated with each file. I recommend you name the file with your actual book title (e.g., *Secrets Every Author Should Know*). Including the author's name along with the book title is suggested if you are publishing under multiple names or are uploading as part of a publishing cooperative with multiple authors. For example: **Maggie Lynch Secrets Every Author Should Know**. The name is displayed as part of your records to make it easy for you to locate the record associated with this registration. So make sure whatever name you select is readily recognizable to you.

It may take a minute or two for the file to upload, depending on the size, so be patient. Once the upload completes you will get a confirmation screen that says: **The following files were successfully uploaded for service request** (followed by a number).

Click on the **Close Window** button at the bottom of the screen to finish the process. You will then receive an email confirming receipt of your uploaded file. Print out the email and save it. I have a file folder marked "Copyright Registration" in which I keep all the emails for each of my books until I receive the actual **Certificate of Registration** in the mail. In this way I have a paper trail of the entire transaction should I need it.

Copyright registration is important. The electronic registration process available at the United States Copyright Office makes it fairly quick and easy. For maximum protection, register every book within three months of its publication.

Chapter Nine
FORMATTING THE EASY WAY

I used to teach classes in formatting for print and ebooks. My personal favorite tool was Jutoh. I still like the tool and use it myself. However, I realized that for most authors the whole concept of formatting was a huge technical challenge. Most indie authors write one, or maybe two books a year. This means when it comes to formatting, it is something they only do twice a year. That means they've forgotten half of what they did before.

Fortunately, it doesn't have to be that way anymore. For those who are not technically inclined there are now ways to get your book formatted for free or little cost, depending on how much customization you want.

Draft2Digital to the Rescue

The number one way I recommend getting "free" easy formatting is using Draft2Digital (http://draft2digital.com). Draft2Digital (D2D) is an aggregator. This means that you can use them to distribute books for you to any vendors where you don't want to or can't load directly. I use them for loading to Apple, Nook, Tolino, 24 Symbols, ScribD, and other distributors. I still load to Amazon and Kobo myself. I used to load everywhere myself, but I no longer find it worthwhile. Of course, there is a cost for this distribution. They take 10% of your earnings. So, what does this have to do with formatting?

Unlike other aggregators, they don't have a big style sheet for how to prepare your book in Microsoft Word or HTML. You simply take your Word document and make it look how you want it to look and then load it to D2D. In fact, the more simple your word document the better. For example, using some bolded chapter heads and subheads and a slightly different font size is enough.

D2D runs it through their conversion engine and with some nice little backend tricks, out comes a very nice EPUB file and a MOBI (Kindle) file. You have the chance to look it over online and approve it for publication or not. If your particular Microsoft Word document, or text document, or Open Office document didn't quite turn out the file you want, their support is excellent at helping you get it in the shape it needs to be.

90% of the authors I've referred to them are amazed at how beautiful their ebook files look. And the best part is that once the file is generated you can also download it and use it elsewhere yourself. Want to sell direct from your website? You can use the beautiful file they created for you. Want to load the EPUB file to a place where D2D doesn't distribute (e.g., All Romance Ebooks or Bublish)? No problem. They are happy for you to do that. There is no D2D copyright page requirement, no special DRM or other code to stop you from doing that.

As if building a functional ebook file that you can use wasn't enough, they will also be happy to build you a print book file in PDF. Sure, it's a one size fits all template, but then so are all the books that people create for Createspace using their template. It's still beautiful, has pagination, and everything you need. Oh, and the cost? Free.

Ah...but there's more. (Sounds like an infomercial right, but it's really true) D2D also allows you to create common sections that you are going to use every time and have them automatically included in your file without you having to create them in Word at all. You pick and choose what you want to use and what you don't want to use.

The sections include:

- Title Page generated from the book data you enter
- Copyright Page generated from the book data
- Also By Page which features all the other books you have loaded at D2D by series
- New Release Email Notification Signup
- Teaser Page that you design
- About the Author Page
- About the Publisher Page

Some of these pages you can choose where they are placed—front of book, back of book, both places. Truly, this is the first file generator I've seen that allows you to concentrate on getting the manuscript in the shape you want and not have to worry about much else.

Use the Vendor Conversion Engines

If you don't choose to use D2D, another free option is to use the vendor conversion engines. Three out of the five major vendors have conversion engines themselves: Amazon, Kobo, and Nook. Like D2D, you upload a Word document and it converts it to the file used by that vendor—MOBI for Amazon, EPUB for Kobo and Nook.

The problem with this approach is that each vendor has some problems with its conversion process, depending on the shape of your Word document. Consequently, each vendor also has a formatting document it wants you to follow before uploading your Word file. Of the three, the most reliable is Amazon, with Kobo coming in second and Nook pretty unreliable.

Some authors upload their file to Amazon to get the MOBI file done, and then put it in Calibre—a free downloadable software (http://calibre.com) to convert to EPUB. I do NOT recommend this. The EPUB file that Calibre creates is not standard and can't be validated. This means it probably won't work to load to Apple, Nook, or Kobo. Calibre is designed for you to be able to read files in different formats using it's native reader.

What If I don't Want to Look Like Everyone Else?

I understand this. I'm a special snowflake too (big smile). If you don't want to take the easy way and let D2D do it for you, or take a chance on the vendors, then there are two choices: 1) Pay someone to create the files for you, or 2) Learn to use some of the software tools and do it yourself. Your choice. Your time. Your money.

Pay Someone. Depending on how much customization you want. The going rate for creating ebook files is between $50 and $100 on average. For the $50 price you get the one size fits all service. Most ebook file producers use a particular program they like and have a specific way in which you must provide your manuscript. The $50 price is no customization, but there is a guarantee that the file will validate at all vendors. The price goes up if you want more customization and/or you have images, illustrations, tables that need to be included.

The price for a print book file runs from $125 to $300 and can be more. Again, depending on the amount of customization you need and if the content contains something other than narrative. Most services that do print book creation use Adobe InDesign.

Learn To Use The Software. There are many software tools to help you create ebook files. The most popular ones are:

Legend Maker (Runs on MAC only $25) – a solid EPUB file builder. It does not create MOBI files for Kindle. For a basic narrative book, it does a good job and a number of professional ebook formatters have used it for years. https://itunes.apple.com/us/app/legend-maker/id459521026?mt=12

Vellum (Runs on Mac Only $30 per title or $199 for unlimited use for ebook formatting. If you want both ebook and print formatting it is $299). https://vellum.pub/

I began using Vellum in early 2017. Once I had 20 titles, I realized I needed something that was faster and still created beautiful books. I'd heard raves from other authors, but found them hard to believe. It turns out the raves are well-deserved.

It is the "gold standard" for creating beautiful books in a quick and easy way. It allows for special fonts, including drop caps, decorative scene breaks, ease of adding images, an ability to easily create boxed sets, and all of this is shown in live preview mode so you can see what it looks like.

You import a Microsoft Word document. You don't need to worry a lot about formatting except to have a common way to delineate chapters (e.g., Heading font or bold). Once the document is imported, Vellum shows you how it thinks those chapters and pages look. You have options to rearrange the order, add or remove sections, copy and paste from one section to another, and other functionality.

When you have the book looking the way you want, you click the GENERATE button and Vellum creates a MOBI file for Kindle and five slightly different EPUB files in vendor-specific formats. It will generate a generic EPUB file, as well as vendor-specific EPUB files for Kobo, Nook, Apple, and Google Play. Though you can easily load the "generic" EPUB file to all five of those vendors, having them separate does allow you to add vendor-specific book links for that platform if you like to load direct. If you use an aggregator to distribute your files, like Draft2Digital or Smashwords or StreetLib, then loading the generic EPUB file is the best.

UPDATE: On June 1, 2017 Vellum offered an upgrade to add the ability to create a PRINT file. I immediately upgraded and all I can say is WOW! This will save me hours and days of formatting work. With the ease of a couple clicks, Vellum will take the file you created for your ebooks and make it into a print-ready PDF file that can be loaded to Createspace or Ingram Spark. It will have all the stylized properties you selected previously formatted in your print book. In addition, Vellum will set the margins, add headers and footers (including your name and the book title on facing pages) and paginate appropriately. Because of the template, Vellum already knows not to put page numbers on things like front matter and back matter.

I had three ebooks I had created in Vellum previously, now waiting for me to format for print. In a matter of 5 minutes I had converted all three of them to PDFs ready to be loaded to Createspace and Ingram Spark.

Reasons NOT to use Vellum. Of course nothing is perfect. Anytime you use an automated formatting system there are trade offs. You can decide whether the trade offs are worth it.

The biggest complaint about Vellum is that it only runs on a MAC and the vast majority of authors use PCs. At this writing Vellum has no plans to create a PC version. So, those who want to use this software currently have two choices. Buy a MAC or use Mac in Cloud. Mac in Cloud is a virtual MAC that allows you to use all kinds of Mac software in a cloud environment. You pay by the hour. See macincloud.com

The second complaint has to do with inflexibility of interior design. The reason Vellum is fast with the formatting is that they have five templates from which to choose. You cannot add new templates, and you cannot change the templates design. If you are the type of person who wants a unique design or enjoys tweaking some things just for you, then Vellum is not the right product for you.

Jutoh (Mac or PC $40). http://jutoh.com I'm personally a huge Jutoh fan, and had used this product for six years until I switched to Vellum in January 2017. Jutoh provides a product that allows the user to have more control over the look and feel of the book, and of the types of metadata to include. You can use it out of the box without understanding any coding. However, the more technical user can really take advantage of its capabilities and make it do most anything you want.

The most important aspect of Jutoh is that the software developer definitely keeps up with changes in epub standards and he is always willing to offer email support if you have a problem. Jutoh does create both EPUB and MOBI (Kindle) files as well as about 9 other types that are used on older readers or PCs and phones. It does come with a good user manual to help authors understand the many capabilities of the product.

PRINT BOOK FORMATTING

For print book creation, the #1 software choice for professionals is ***Adobe InDesign***. It is an amazing piece of software that gives you full control over every aspect of the book. However, it is expensive and complex. The learning curve is long. Most professional contractors you might hire to do print book interiors use Adobe InDesign.

The average author doing her own formatting uses Microsoft Word and creates a template design that she likes by defining styles and using those styles consistently throughout the document. This requires a thorough understanding of Microsoft Word formatting, style use, and template use.

Alternatively, you can download a template from a vendor. Createspace has a template for interiors that you can download and install in your copy of Microsoft Word. It is basic, but it works and doesn't have a lot of fancy options.

You can also purchase a Microsoft Word template from someone like The Book Designer. http://www.bookdesigntemplates.com/ These templates have already made all the style decisions for you. The template provides a Word document with headers, footers, pagination, font choices, spacing etc. already in place. All you need to do is add the content. These really are great templates and the pricing is quite reasonable considering the amount of time you can save setting up this yourself. You can preview them at the website and select a style you like.

The only caveat to the template option is that you must be comfortable with using Microsoft Words advance features of styles. Even with the template already set up, it is easy to get lost and to accidentally make formatting changes to the styles if you aren't really conversant with how it works.

As with anything you do yourself in your self-publishing journey, you need to weigh your desire for control and making something beautiful with the time and/or money it takes to get to that point. This evaluation is different for each author.

I am comfortable with technology and so I have always done my own formatting for print and ebooks. However, every time I consider this task, I have to make decisions about how much time I'm willing to put in to the interior design of my books and what I'm willing to sacrifice to get it done more quickly. I do want them to look professional, but I also know that the most important part is what the reader gets out of the book. It may look nice to have fancy headers, and drop caps, and special dividers. But that doesn't really enhance the reading experience for most people. With Vellum I have now found an easy compromise for me for my ebooks and print. However, you may make other choices.

For the vast majority of authors I know, when they discovered how well the D2D engine worked, they were more than happy to give up their formatting software and the time it took them to make beautiful books. They are now letting D2D handle all the formatting for them.

For the few who want something really special or unique, they pay a formatter to deal with it or allocate extra hours to create beautiful books in software like InDesign. They consider it a cost of doing business. It's always time or money that is the trade off.

Chapter Ten
DISTRIBUTION

Now that you have created a well-crafted story or non-fiction work, have added front and back matter, decided on formatting and created the print and ebook files you need, it's time to get the book distributed. The next book in this series, Secrets to Pricing and Distribution, goes into great detail as to all the options for distributing your book. It also provides step-by-step instructions for loading to each of the major vendors, as well as to D2D.

For this section in this indie publishing basics book, we are going to discuss the foundations of distribution in order to set you up to make some choices on what is the best way for you to get your book to all the markets that are important for you.

Print Book Distribution

The Print-on-Demand (POD) printing technology is primarily owned and operated by two large companies: Ingram, through its Lightning Source subsidiary; and Amazon, through its CreateSpace subsidiary. The vast majority of indie authors use one of these two vendors.

In addition to these two large distributors, there is Lulu

http://lulu.com which has been around a very long time and has a great reputation. There are also print services company like Xlibris, and Outskirts Press who really make their money on providing the author book creation services—formatting, cover design, etc. for a package deal fee. For the purposes of this book, I am focusing on CreateSpace and Ingram Spark, as they are the most used by indie authors today.

Let's begin by comparing CreateSpace and Lightning Source. Both are reputable companies that produce library-quality books using a print-on-demand model (i.e., books are printed and shipped to fulfill customer orders). While some services overlap, each company has its strengths and weaknesses. Your preference depends largely on your needs and objectives. In my opinion, the end product is equal between these two sources. In fact, CreateSpace often uses Lighting Source's POD printers when volume overwhelms its own network in the U.S. And for Expanded Distribution (outside the U.S.) CreateSpace uses Ingram for all POD printing.

Let's look at the primary differences between the two:
CreateSpace

- Nice array of trim sizes
- Laminate or Matte cover finish available
- Paperback only
- Setup fee is free.
- Proof copy is your cost for the book. Typical author cost for a 360 page 6 x 9 inch book is approximately $5.00
- You can make changes and reload the book any time for free.
- Expanded distribution through Ingram is free
- Royalties are 35% for Amazon sales and 25% for sales through Expanded distribution

Ingram Spark

- Wider range of trim sizes

- Choice of laminate or matte finish on cover
- Choice of paperback or hard cover
- Setup fee is $49
- Proof copy cost is price of book plus shipping and handling
- Change fee is $40
- Author price for a 360 page 6 x 9 inch book is approximately $5.45
- Fee for distribution through Ingram is $12 per book per year in the US and an additional $12.00 per book per year in the UK.
- Royalties vary depending on author choices for discount, range from 30% to 40%

The above are the basic setup and distribution costs. In addition there are other differences that may impact an author's decision, particularly if you wish to work with a large number of bookstores.

CreateSpace sets the wholesale discount at 20% at the CreateSpace store, 40% at Amazon, and 60% in expanded distribution. Most small bookstores refuse to order print books from order print books through Ingram, and their discount is only 25%. This means they won't stock, but will order upon customer request.

Ingram Spark allows you to choose the wholesale discount of either 40% or 55%. If you choose 40% then the bookstores discount is only 25% (like CreateSpace through Ingram). If you set the discount for 55%, the bookstore discount is 40%, which MAY encourage them to stock the book for special events or signings.

Three other things to consider are turn-around for proof copies, time it takes to get in distribution once you put it on sale, and over all customer service. Proof copies of the book are handled differently with each vendor.

CreateSpace offers two choices: reviewing an online proof copy of both the interior and cover; or having a copy of the finished book mailed to you for proofing. The cost to you is the cost of the book plus shipping. Mailing time varies based on what you are willing to pay for shipping. The least expensive is UPS ground, which is guaranteed delivery in seven to ten days.

Ingram Spark also provides online proof copies; or having a copy of the finished book mailed to you for proofing. The cost to you is the cost of the book plus shipping and handling. Shipping is charged on three-day express delivery, so twice the cost of CreateSpace lowest option.

Time to distribution is dependent on where your book is being distributed. CreateSpace electronically transfers your finalized book information immediately to all Amazon stores you've elected. Making your book available in the expanded distribution network takes approximately a month to six weeks. It appears at Barnes & Noble within a week, but other bookstores take up to a month. That's because the files are sent to Ingram and Baker & Taylor for loading and then to Lightning Source for POD printing.

Ingram Spark distribution to all bookstores supported by Ingram appears in the catalog with 24 hours, at Amazon usually within one week, and displayed in other online stores in two weeks.

Customer service is also markedly different between the two companies. Ingram Spark provides no way to contact support except through their internal ticketing system. There is an expectation on their part that you'll understand how to navigate the site, what all the selection options and terms mean, and how to upload a print-ready book without mistakes. (NOTE: a Word Document saved as a PDF is not a print-ready file and will not be accepted by Ingram Spark. Their preferred software for generating print-ready books is Adobe InDesign).

As a result of their expectation that you will know how to create an acceptable file, customer support is slow to respond to individual author difficulties with the system. An average turn-around time is three days. If there is a problem with your file, they identify what it is and leave it to you to fix it and reload. Or you can pay them to fix it. Payments range from $10 to $40 depending on the problem.

CreateSpace, on the other hand, has instant phone and email support 24 hours a day. Is CreateSpace sometimes frustrating to deal with? Sure. Not all reps are created equal. Customer support groups have a diversity of talent and people skills among the staff. You can load a Word Document saved as PDF, and CreateSpace will convert it to the appropriate print-ready file at no extra cost.

After two years of analyzing the difference in sales going through Ingram Spark vs. CreateSpace, I've chosen to use CreateSpace for all my POD printing needs. I did not see a significant uptake in books at bookstores because of the additional discount (I set it for 55%). Nor did I see any significant increase in print book sales to offset the additional per book cost ($49 + $12 for catalog inclusion) and the extensive additional time to create a print-ready book outside of Microsoft Word.

Ebook Distribution

We've previously discussed that there are two ways to distribute ebooks. One is for the author to upload direct to vendors. The other is to upload to an aggregator like D2D and let them distribute to vendors for you.

Unlike print books where the majority of POD printing is handled by only two vendors, ebooks have a plethora of distribution options. In fact, it seems that a new vendor pops up weekly. The five largest distributors are Amazon, Apple, Kobo, Google, and Barnes & Noble Nook. All, except Nook, distribute to many countries around the world. Nook is now only in the U.S.

In addition to these large distributors, there are hundreds of other possibilities. Some are genre specific such as ARe (All Romance ebooks), while others are simply e-commerce portals that purport to offer better discoverability than the large distribution options. There are at least 40 vendors that do provide a means for you to upload directly. There is another hundred or more that you can only reach through an aggregator (Draft2Digital, Smashwords, StreetLib, Book Baby, Vearsa, etc.) Though it would appear the best approach is to have your book everywhere, the reality of that kind of distribution makes it costly in terms of both time and money. The key is to determine where your readers are and how best to reach them.

Let's look at the big five ebook distributors and their market potential first.

Vendor	Country Access	Royalty payment*	Payment Terms
Amazon	12	35%, 70%	60 days
Apple	51	70%	32 days
Kobo	190	65%	60 days
Google	Worldwide	65%	32 days
B&N Nook	1	65%	60 days

* Amazon pays 35% on books that are less than $2.99 or more than $9.99, and 70% on books that fall in the $2.99 to $9.99 range. Also several of the countries where Amazon distributes (e.g., Brazil, India, Japan, Mexico) only pay 35% unless you are exclusive to them.

Though it is true for most authors that the majority of sales are with Amazon, one needs to carefully consider if they want to be exclusive. Let's look at the pros and cons.

Feature	Amazon	All other vendors
Category Selection	2	3-5
Coupons	0	Unlimited
Exclusivity	Required for some benefits	Not required
File Types	MOBI	EPUB
Free book price change	5 days available with exclusivity, or approved in advanced for permafree	Available anytime for any period

In the *Secrets of Pricing and Distribution* book, I go into detail about each of these vendors, how to load to them and how to use different pricing and metadata strategies. The key for you at this point is to keep in mind there is more than Amazon and is it worth it for you to be exclusive to one vendor and miss out on the opportunities other vendors provide.

Aggregators

As discussed previously, aggregators provide a means to distribute to the major players and beyond. Prior to 2015, I would have said there is no reason to use an aggregator to distribute to the main vendors (Amazon, Google, Kobo, Apple, Nook). I would have said that going direct gets you much better traction with each vendor and you can build up a network with merchandisers and marketers at each one. I've changed my mind on that.

For the vast majority of indie authors, there is no disadvantage to using an aggregator with all vendors outside of the 10%-15% fee they take from sales. Major aggregators can now work with merchandisers on your behalf. They can sometimes get deals that are only offered to the most successful authors. The ease of loading your book once and having it distributed everywhere is something to consider. The ease of getting reports for all sales in one place, instead of having to check at each vendor is also nice.

The downside of having an aggregator load everywhere is that you lose some control. Having one book distributed everywhere through an aggregator also means that you treat all vendors alike—same pricing, same promotional periods, same look and feel. You can load multiple copies of the same book at an aggregator and designate it the Kobo book or the Apple book. However, in my opinion, if you are going to that much trouble you are better off loading direct.

If you like the control of loading to each vendor yourself, networking with merchandisers, and being able to run promotions, change pricing, do linking to vendor-specific titles with each vendor then you need to load direct.

I used to load direct to each of the big five distributors. I tracked sales with software in order to get all information in one place, and I was minimally successful with networking and finding merchandisers at each vendor. I only used aggregators to reach markets I could not reach on my own like Tolino, Overdrive, and some subscription service markets. In late 2015 I made the decision to use aggregators for everything except Amazon and Kobo. I reserved those two markets for continued direct loads because that is where I had built up the most metadata, sales records, and relationships.

Even if you choose to load direct to the major vendors, there are still markets you cannot reach as a solo indie publisher unless you have a large backlist of books AND good facility with a variety of upload techniques (e.g., FTP, CSV files, coding metadata fields, etc.). An aggregator takes care of this for you.

There are numerous companies claiming to be the best aggregator for you. Most of them make their money off author services rather than distribution (formatting, marketing packages, cover designs, etc.). Unless you want an all-in-one package company, I would recommend staying away from these. Some good aggregators charge a monthly fee for distribution plus a percentage of sales. You need to decide if the additional markets they provide are worth that investment. For the vast majority of indie authors I would say it is not worth it.

There are three aggregators that serve the majority of indie authors: Smashwords and Draft2Digital (D2D) are based in the United States; and StreetLib is in Italy. Smashwords has been around for nearly two decades and has been a great proponent of self-publishing all of that time. D2D is the new kid on the block, opening in 2013, but has garnered huge support among indie authors. StreetLib is even newer, founded in 2014, but has been quick to expand its distributor platforms particularly into non-English speaking countries.

An advantage of being new is that the software platform doesn't have to be backwards compatible or have all the legacy processes to keep going. A disadvantage of being new is that they don't have as many relationships already built which means some markets aren't yet available. Below is a quick breakdown of the key components of the platforms.

Feature	Smashwords	D2D	StreetLib
Input Formats	.doc, epub	.doc, .docx, .rtf, epub	epub
Commission	15% on Smashwords, 10% net all others	10% all platforms	10% all platforms
Who Formats	You	They Do	You
ISBN	Free	Free	
Coupons	Yes for their bookstore	No	Yes for their bookstore
Distribution	Apple, Kobo, Nook, Overdrive, Blio, Baker & Taylor, Gardners Inktera	Apple, Kobo, Nook, Inktera, Tolino, ScribD, 24 Symbols, and CreateSpace	Amazon, Apple, Kobo, Nook, Google Play, Overdrive, Tolino, Bookmate, 15 major country stores in Italy, Spain, and Latin America, Stores in Turkey and Poland as well as library distribution in those countries
Preorders	Yes	Yes	No
Payment Schedule	Quarterly	Monthly	Quarterly after ~ $30 minimum threshold
Support	Email and ticketing	Phone, email, & ticketing	Email and ticketing

The downside of having an aggregator load everywhere is that you lose some control. Having one book distributed everywhere through an aggregator also means that you treat all vendors alike—same pricing, same promotional periods, same look and feel. You can load multiple copies of the same book at an aggregator and designate it the Kobo book or the Apple book. However, in my opinion, if you are going to that much trouble you are better off loading direct.

If you like the control of loading to each vendor yourself, networking with merchandisers, and being able to run promotions, change pricing, do linking to vendor-specific titles with each vendor then you need to load direct.

I used to load direct to each of the big five distributors. I tracked sales with software in order to get all information in one place, and I was minimally successful with networking and finding merchandisers at each vendor. I only used aggregators to reach markets I could not reach on my own like Tolino, Overdrive, and some subscription service markets. In late 2015 I made the decision to use aggregators for everything except Amazon and Kobo. I reserved those two markets for continued direct loads because that is where I had built up the most metadata, sales records, and relationships.

Even if you choose to load direct to the major vendors, there are still markets you cannot reach as a solo indie publisher unless you have a large backlist of books AND good facility with a variety of upload techniques (e.g., FTP, CSV files, coding metadata fields, etc.). An aggregator takes care of this for you.

There are numerous companies claiming to be the best aggregator for you. Most of them make their money off author services rather than distribution (formatting, marketing packages, cover designs, etc.). Unless you want an all-in-one package company, I would recommend staying away from these. Some good aggregators charge a monthly fee for distribution plus a percentage of sales. You need to decide if the additional markets they provide are worth that investment. For the vast majority of indie authors I would say it is not worth it.

There are three aggregators that serve the majority of indie authors: Smashwords, Draft2Digital (D2D) (both in the United States) and StreetLib in Italy. Smashwords has been around for nearly two decades and has been a great proponent of self-publishing all of that time. D2D is the new kid on the block, opening in 2013, but has garnered huge support among indie authors. StreetLib is even newer, founded in 2014, but has been quick to expand its distributor platforms particularly into non-English speaking countries.

An advantage of being new is that the software platform doesn't have to be backwards compatible or have all the legacy processes to keep going. A disadvantage of being new is that they don't have as many relationships already built which means some markets aren't yet available. Below is a quick breakdown of the key components of the platforms.

Analysis

Each aggregator has its pros and cons:

For **distribution**, Smashword has the largest library presence with four major library distributors. However, StreetLib does have the largest ebook distribution partnership with Overdrive, and has everyone beat for both library and bookstore distribution in non-English speaking countries—particularly Italy, Spain, Mexico, and Latin America. D2D is still building their distribution list. Their presence in Tolino is huge for the European market, which Smashwords does not have. D2D also has distribution with a variety of German and French distributors as well as subscription service platforms.

With ease of use, D2D is the king of all three platforms. The design is pretty and intuitive, easier to use and navigate. And the biggie is they do the formatting for you. The StreetLib platform is easier to navigate than Smashwords, but it has some quirks and it does require a validated EPUB file. They do no conversion at all.

Both Smashwords and StreetLib have their own bookstore, which provides one more discoverability outlet. However, outside of the use of coupons, most authors report little to no sales via these bookstores.

For regular payment D2D is the winner in that they pay monthly with no minimum requirements. Both Smashwords and StreetLib pay quarterly. StreetLib does require a $30 threshold before payments will commence.

So whom do you choose? The good news is you don't have to choose just one. I have chosen D2D as my primary aggregator because of its ease of use, monthly payments, and its continued upgrading of the platform with nice options like those mentioned in the formatting section of this book.

I do want to be in libraries. Even though D2D says they are working on getting a contract with Overdrive, I'm not willing wait right now. So, I am going to StreetLib in order to get into Overdrive. While there, I am also taking advantage of their special country distributions into Italy, Spain, Mexico, and Latin America. Though my books are currently only in English there are possibilities of English-speaking people in those countries looking for books.

UPDATE: Rakuten, the parent company of Kobo Books, purchased Overdrive in late 2016. It is likely that eventually there will be some agreement around how Kobo books are placed in Overdrive. Six months after the purchase there have been no announcements or further word on that transition. One can only hope it will become easier for authors to get into Overdrive in the future.

As with all things, the choice is yours. Look into each of these to see which works best for you. What are the overriding elements for each platform? Or, if you are happy with loading direct to the majors and that's all you want, then no need to use an aggregator at all.

There are also other aggregators with good reputations, like Book Baby. However, you pay a premium for those services in terms of upfront cost and the commissions they take are significantly larger than the ones mentioned above.

Chapter Eleven
WHAT'S NEXT?

Now that you have the tools to take your manuscript to publication, the next steps in your publishing journey are to learn the specifics of distributors and how their metadata is used for discoverability. You can do that through *Secrets of Pricing and Distribution*. Then hone your marketing skills with *Secrets of Effective Author Marketing*. Finally, if you want to make writing and publishing your career, check out *Secrets to Building the Career You Want*.

Need a little more handholding and mentoring with these steps? Please check out my online Indie Publishing Series video series at http://aww-on-the-go.teachable.com/

These courses provide additional handouts, cheat sheets, one-on-

one discussions and troubleshooting, as well as live web-conference demonstrations and coaching sessions.

Finally, I maintain a mailing list of authors who are interested in getting more information. I occasionally send out articles, at no cost, about what I'm doing and what I'm learning that's new. I also share new releases of my books geared toward indie authors.

You can sign up for that mailing list on my website http://maggielynch.com

ABOUT THE AUTHOR

Maggie is the author of 20+ published books, as well as more than 30 short stories and numerous non-fiction articles. She is also the founder of Windtree Press, an independent publishing cooperative. Her love of lifelong-learning has garnered degrees in psychology, counseling, computer science, and education; and led to opportunities to consult in Europe, Australia, and the Middle East. Since 2013, Maggie has enjoyed the luxury of writing full-time. Her adult fiction spans romance, suspense, and SF titles under the name Maggie Jaimeson. She writes YA Fantasy under the name Maggie Faire. Her non-fiction titles are found under Maggie McVay Lynch.

For more information:
maggielynch.com

Visit us at http://windtreepress.com

www.ingramcontent.com/pod-product-compliance
Lightning Source LLC
Chambersburg PA
CBHW071735080526
44588CB00013B/2045